Introduction to the US-American Legal System
for German-Speaking Lawyers and Law Students

Vol. 1

W0369934

2005

Dr. Alexander Dörrbecker, LL.M.
Attorney at Law (New York)
Referent im Bundesministerium der Justiz, Berlin

Dr. Oliver Rothe, LL.M.
Rechtsanwalt in Düsseldorf

ALPMANN UND SCHMIDT Juristische Lehrgänge Verlagsges. mbH & Co. KG
48149 Münster, Annette-Allee 35, 48001 Postfach 1169, Telefon (0251) 98109-33/28
AS-Online: www.alpmann-schmidt.de

Dr. Dörrbecker, Alexander
Dr. Rothe, Oliver

Introduction to the US-American Legal System, Vol. 1
for German-Speaking Lawyers and Law Students

2. Auflage 2005
ISBN 3-89476-799-5

Preface

As the first edition has been well received, we are happy to provide you with an updated and completely reviewed second edition.
Again, we would like to give you an introduction to a legal system that is new to the German law student and lawyer. The U.S. legal system is based on many completely different ideas and concepts compared to the German system. However, in the course of the discussion we will find problems and issues that are familiar to us.
This book is not a treatise on comparative law. We hardly will make reference to the German legal system.
What does this introduction contain? In this volume we will give a general introduction at the beginning. The introduction is followed by a broad survey of constitutional law and the law of contracts. As in most legal systems, the constitution is the basis upon which to understand the underlying ideas and main legal problems. It also gives an idea of the different powers established by the Constitution. The law of contracts is the main area of U.S. law that gives an insight into the common law principles, because in this field the classical approaches of the common law still apply. In comparison the law of sales is mainly governed by a statute: the Uniform Commercial Code (U.C.C.). However, we will deal with the law of sales in volume II.
Volume II will also contain the law of torts, corporate law, and procedural questions that seem to be very important for the practice of a M & A and general corporate lawyer.
The case-based method has proven to be successful. As the U.S. is a common law jurisdiction country, cases play a decisive role. Thus, you will find many summarized cases. This approach has two main advantages, firstly, you can generally keep legal problems better in mind if you can think of concrete names and cases. Secondly, the cases will give you an insight in the way American lawyers think. You will see that it is often different from our way of thinking.
The cases are surrounded by text that will help you to understand what the court decided and why it decided in that way. Additionally, you will find diagrams at the end of many sections. These diagrams sum up what we have explained in each previous section and they make it easier to keep in mind the material discussed.
Sometimes we will add text boxes containing background information about justices, presidents or legal terms. We think it is important to put court decisions in a historical and personal context. Unfortunately, these text boxes can only be very brief but they invite you to do some additional reading to gain a better understanding of the U.S. legal system.
The special feature of this series is that this book deals with a foreign legal system and it is written in English. Alpmann und Schmidt has already published in this series the "Introduction into the English Civil Law" by Prof. Dr. Rainer Wörlen whose idea it was to create marginal notes to give translation aids.
If you have any comments, questions or remarks about the structure or content of the outline please contact us: as.info@alpmann-schmidt.de

Münster, February 2005

Alexander Dörrbecker
Oliver Rothe

Chapter One

Chapter Two

Bibliography

Alces/Hansford	Sales, Leases and Bulk Transfers (1993)
Barron/Dienes/McCormick	Constitutional Law: Principles and Policy (6th ed., 2000)
Corbin	*Contracts (1993)*
Craswell/Schwartz	Foundations on Contract Law (1994)
Crump	*Cases and Materials on Constitutional Law 4th ed., 2002)*
Ely	Democracy and Distrust: A Theory on Judicial Review (1981)
Farnsworth	Selection for Contracts (2003)
Farnsworth	Contracts (2001)
Gilmore	The Death of Contract (1974)
King e.a.	Sales Law (1997)
Kronman/Posner	The Economics of Contract Law (1979)
Lawrence/Henning	Understanding Sales and Leases of Goods (1996)
Macaulay e.a.	Contracts: Law in Action (1995)
Marks/Cooper	State Constitutional Law in a Nutshell (2003)
McGovern/Lawrence	Contracts and Sales: Cases and Problems (1993)
Murray	Contracts: Cases and Materials (5th ed., 2000)
Nowak/Rotunda	Constitutional Law (7th ed., 2004)
Redlich/Attanasio/Goldstein	Constitutional Law (4th ed., 2001)
Scott/Powell/Leon	Contract Law and Theory (2nd ed., 1993)
Sunstein	The Partial Constitution (1994)
Tribe	American Constitutional Law (3rd ed., 2003)
Wechsler	Principles, Politics and Fundamental Law (1961)
Williston	A Treatise on the Law of Contracts (4th ed., 1990)

The life of the law has not been logic: it has been experience. The seed of every new growth within its sphere has been a felt necessity. The form of continuity has been kept up by reasonings purporting to reduce everything to a logical sequence; but that form is nothing but the evening dress which the newcomer puts on to make itself presentable according to conventional requirements. The important phenomenon is the man underneath it, not the coat; the justice and reasonableness of a decision, not its consistency with previously held views. No one will every have a truly philosophic mastery over the law who does not habitually consider the forces outside of it which have made it what it is.

– Oliver Wendell Holmes, Jr., review of "A Selection of Cases on the Law of Contracts. . .", 2d ed., by Christoper C. Langdell, American Law Review 14 (1880), 233.

Chapter One

Introduction

Part 1: Common Law System

The USA is a common law country.
The term "common law" evokes confusion and uncertainty. — erzeugen
The term "common law" may refer to any of the following: — sich beziehen auf

A. Common Law as Differentiated From Civil Law

A "common law" system relies heavily on **court precedent in formal adjudications**. In the American common law system, even when a statute is at issue, judicial determinations in earlier court cases are extremely critical to the court's resolution of the matter before it. **Civil law systems rely less on court precedent and more on codes**, which explicitly provide rules of decision for many specific disputes. When a judge needs to go beyond the letter of a code in disposing of a dispute, the judge's resolution will not become binding or perhaps even relevant in subsequent determinations involving other parties.

relies – precedent	beruhen – Präzedenzfall
determinations	Feststellung
critical	entscheidend
resolution	Beschluss
codes – provide	Gesetzestext – vorschreiben
disputes	Streitigkeit
become binding	bindend werden
subsequent	nachfolgend

B. Case Law

Common law may refer to **"judge-made" law**, otherwise known as case law. Cases are legal determinations based on a set of particular facts involving parties with a genuine interest in the controversy.

determinations	Feststellung
genuine	eigen

I. Several General Types of Case Law

1. Pure Decisional Case Law

Court called upon to decide cases **on the bases of prior court decisions (precedent)** and/or policy and a sense of inherent fairness. In cases of pure decisional law, there is no applicable statute or constitutional provision that applies.

policy	Taktik, Politik, Grundsatz
inherent	innewohnend

This type of decisional law is what is referred to as "judicially-created doctrine". Historically, the term "case law" referred to certain areas of law (e.g., torts, property) that began as judge-made, or pure decisional law. | Deliktsrecht – Sachenrecht

2. Case Law Based on Constitutional Provisions

Court can be called upon to consider whether a particular statute or governmental action is consistent with the United States Constitution or a particular state constitution. Court interpretation may rely upon prior decisional law interpreting the same or some other constitutional provisions. | in Übereinstimmung mit | Auslegung – vorhergehend | Bestimmung

3. Case Law Based on Statutory Provisions

Court called upon to interpret a statute. Court interpretation may rely upon prior decisional law interpreting the same or similar statute. | Gesetz

Part 2: Making of the Constitution

The document that underlies legal and political life in the USA is the Constitution.
The United States Constitution was established on **September 17, 1787**. The founders of the Constitution were delegates appointed by the state legislatures to represent each state's welfare. They had first convened in the Philadelphia statehouse as a quorum of 55 delegates on May 25, 1787. Of the thirteen original states, only Rhode Island declined to participate. The group's express original purpose was to **revise the Articles of Confederation**, the nation's first constitution that was established in 1781 during the Revolutionary War with Great Britain. | entstehen, ausarbeiten | Gründer, Väter | ernennen | zusammentreffen | ablehnen | überarbeiten

A. The Consitutional Convention of 1787

The State of Virginia called a convention in Annapolis, Maryland, in 1786; however, only five states were represented. **Alexander Hamilton** brilliantly saved the convention from failure by calling upon Congress to summon all states to be represented at a convention the following year in Philadelphia, Pennsylvania. Thus, the following year, Congress invoked an assembly, authorizing representatives of the Constitutional Convention to address the weaknesses of the Articles of Confederation. The official purpose of the Constitutional Convention of 1787 was to **propose amendments to the Articles of Confederation** but when the convention convened, the delegates realized that they had two general goals in common: to create a republican form as well as a new constitutional form of government. The delegates knew that they would generate heated differences and they did not want to advertise their own dissentions; thus, they conducted their sessions in complete secrecy with armed sentinels posted outside convention doors.

- vertreten
- Misserfolg
- herbeirufen
- bestellen, anrufen
- Zusätze
- versammeln
- republikanische Form
- konstitutionelle Form
- Verschwiegenheit
- Wächter

This important occasion called for the most able men to drop their personal pursuits and come to the aid of their country. The caliber of representatives and participants was extraordinarily high – **Thomas Jefferson** dubbed everyone present as "demigods". **George Washington**, enormously prestigious as "the sword of the (American) revolution", was unanimously elected chairman of the convention. **Benjamin Franklin** added the experience and urbanity of an elder statesman. **James Madison's** contributions were so notable that he was dubbed "the Father of the Constitution". For seventeen weeks, these men discussed plans, such as Virginia's **"large-state plan"**, which proposed that they abolish the Articles of Confederation and create a new form of government, under which representation in both houses of a bicameral (two house) Congress be essentially based on population. New Jersey countered with its **"small-state plan"**, which called for equal representation of the states in a unicameral (one house) Congress (as it was under the Articles of Confederation), regardless of population or size. After prolonged debate, the delegates arrived at the **"Great Compromise"** or "Connecticut Compromise", which formed a new national government with three branches –

- Wünsche, Ziele
- taufen
- Halbgott
- einstimmig
- Erfahrung – Gewandtheit
- bemerkenswert
- abschaffen, aufheben
- Zwei - Kammer -
- Bevölkerung
- gleiche Vertretung
- Ein - Kammer -
- verlängern

executive, legislative and judicial – as a system of **"checks and balances"**. Furthermore, the legislative branch would be bicameral and the number of delegates each state had in the House of Representatives of the legislative branch was to be based on population. The Senate was to be composed of two Senators from each state, regardless of the population of the state. The Convention delegates also decided that the members of the House of Representatives would be elected directly by the people of the states and would serve two-year terms. The members of the Senate would be elected by the state legislatures and would serve six-year terms.

Exekutive –Legislative – Judicative
Bevölkerung
gewählt
Perioden

The new Constitution also provided for a **strong, independent Executive Branch, which included a President and Vice President**. The President had a term of four years to institute his programs though he could be re-elected if his performance garnered sufficient support. The president was to be the commander-in-chief of the military and was to have wide powers of appointment to domestic offices, including Supreme Court judges.

vorsehen
unabhängig
wiederwählen
ansammeln
oberster Befehlsherr
innenpolitisches Amt
Richter des Obersten Gerichtes

The third branch of the new government, the Judicial Branch, had little specific authority. The Judicial Branch included a Supreme Court that had appellate and original jurisdiction. The Legislative Branch controlled all the other courts and jurisdiction.

Macht, Kompetenz
Berufungs –Zuständigkeit in 1. Instanz

B. Ratification

Before the Constitution could take effect, it had to be ratified by at least nine states. Of the original 55 Constitutional Convention delegates, **42 remained to sign the document**. Only three of these 42 refused to sign the Constitution. When the Constitution was presented to the individual states, the founding fathers asserted that the Constitution was not an amendment to the Articles of Confederation, since it established a completely new form of government. They declared that it required approval by two-thirds, or nine, of the states, and therefore the states held ratification conventions. The delegates from the state conventions, who were chosen by voters in each state, approved the new constitution. The new government thus would receive its

ratifizieren
ablehnen
behaupten, beanspruchen,
einführen
verkünden
Ratifizierungsversammlung
erhalten

power from the people rather than from the states. Several states were alarmed that a Bill of Rights was not created, but they were assured that the first Congress would add such a safeguard by amendment.
Thus, in July of 1789, the people of the United States ratified the Constitution and instituted it as the supreme law of the land.

Macht
Grundrechtekatalog – ins Leben rufen
Schutz

Part 3: Structure of Government

The United States is a **federalist system**. The national government has specific, **enumerated powers**, and the fifty sovereign states retain substantial autonomy and authority. Both the national government and each state government is divided into executive, legislative and judicial branches. Written constitutions, both federal and state, form a system of **separated powers, checks and balances among the branches**.

föderalistisch
aufgezählt
souverän
Gewalt
getrennt

Diagram 1

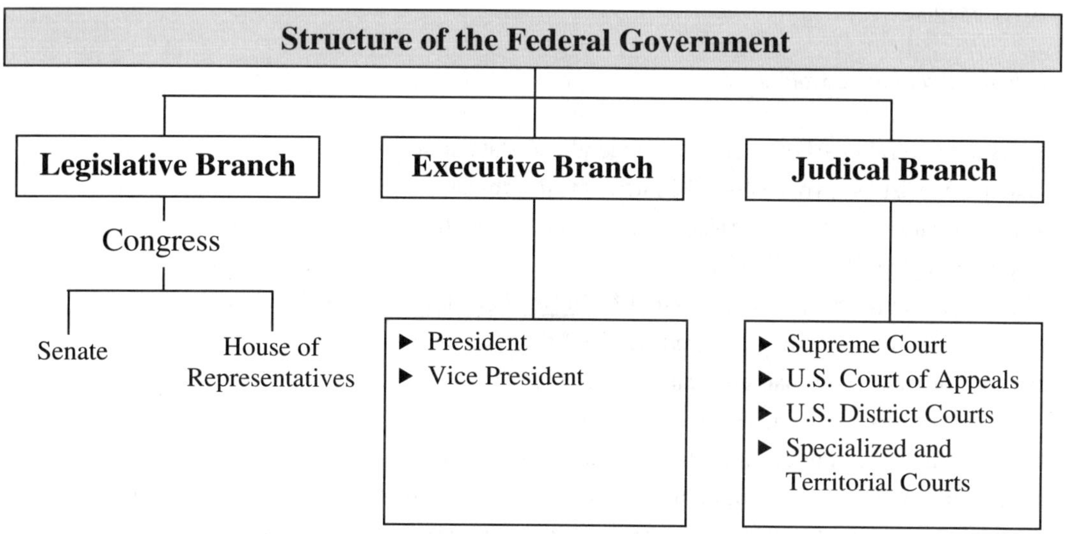

A. Judicial Branch

I. Courts

Article III of the Constitution establishes the federal judicial branch of government. The **Supreme Court** was organized in 1790 with judicial power to review cases arising under the Constitution, the Laws of the United States and treaties. The Constitution gives Congress the authority to create **additional federal courts**. The hierarchical system which evolved is **Courts of Appeal** and lower level trial courts, **Federal District Courts.**

vorsehen
überprüfen – herrühren, stammen
Kompetenz
Bundesgericht
Berufungsgericht –
erstinstanzliches Gericht

The federal courts have the judicial responsibility to rule on the constitutionality of federal laws, to interpret and to apply the laws to resolve disputes. The federal courts have **"limited" jurisdiction** in that they can only decide certain types of cases as determined by Congress or defined in the Constitution. That means the federal courts decide cases interpreting the Constitution, all federal laws, federal regulations and rules, controversies between citizens of different states (diversity jurisdiction) and controversies between states or between the United States and foreign governments.

Verantwortung
Bundesgesetz – anwenden
lösen, überwinden
Verordnung – Regel –
Streitigkeit
ausländische Regierung

1. Federal and State Courts

There are several types of courts. The federal and state court systems consist of two levels of courts: **Trial courts** and **appellate courts**. Cases are **tried** in trial courts. Appellate courts **review** the decisions of the trial courts.

bestehen
verhandeln
überprüfen

The federal court system is divided into **13 judicial circuits**. Eleven of the circuits are numbered. Each of the numbered circuits contains more than one state. The Ninth Circuit, for example, covers California, Oregon, Washington, Idaho, Nevada, Arizona, Alaska, and Hawaii. The 12th and 13th circuits are the District of Columbia Circuit and the Federal Circuit. The Federal Circuit handles appeals in patent cases and Claims Court cases.

Gerichtsbezirk
Patentfall

Each federal circuit has one appellate court. These courts are known as Courts of Appeals or Circuit Courts. The

Supreme Court reviews the decisions of the Courts of Appeals.
Each federal circuit is divided into judicial districts. A district can be as small as one city or as large as an entire state. The trial courts are known as the United States District Courts.

2. The Supreme Court

The Supreme Court of the United States consists of **nine justices** (the Chief Justice and eight Associate Justices) appointed for life by the President with the advice and consent of the Senate. One justice is appointed as the Chief Justice and has additional administrative duties related both to the Supreme Court and to the entire federal court system. Each justice is assigned to one of the courts of appeal for emergency responses.

ernennen – Rat
Zustimmung
Verwaltungsaufgabe
gesamtes Bundesgerichts-
system

a) Session

The Supreme Court meets on the first Monday of October each year and usually continues in session through June. The Supreme Court **receives and disposes of about 5,000 cases each year**, most by a brief decision that the subject matter is either not proper or not of sufficient importance to warrant review by the full court. Cases are heard en banc, which means by all the justices sitting together in open court. Each year the court **decides about 150 cases** of great national importance and interest, and about three-fourths of such decisions are announced in full published opinions.

Sitzungsperiode fortsetzen
erledigen
Verfahrensgegenstand
genügend wichtig
rechtfertigen

verkündet – Meinung

b) Members

Currently, there are the following nine Justices member of the Supreme Court:

- Chief Justice **William H. Rehnquist** (* 1924, Justice since 1972, Chief Justice since 1986), Republican (nominated by Nixon and Reagan)

nominiert

- **John Paul Stevens** (* 1920, Justice since 1975), Republican (nominated by Ford)

- **Sandra Day O'Connor** (*1930, Justice since 1981), Republican (nominated by Reagan)
- **Antonin Scalia** (* 1936, Justice since 1986), Republican (nominated by Reagan)
- **Anthony Kennedy** (* 1936, Justice since 1988), Republican (nominated by Reagan)
- **David Souter** (* 1939, Justice since 1990), Republican (nominated by George H. W. Bush)
- **Clarence Thomas** (* 1948, Justice since 1991), Republican (nominated by George H. W. Bush)
- **Ruth Ginsberg** (* 1933, Justice since 1993), Democrat (nominated by Clinton)
- **Stephen Breyer** (* 1938, Justice since 1994), Democrat (nominated by Clinton)

3. Federal Courts

The federal district courts are the trial courts, both civil and criminal, in the federal system. There are **94 federal district** courts. Each district includes a bankruptcy court. In addition, there are two special trial courts with nationwide jurisdiction over international trade/customs, Court of International Trade, and the Court of Federal Claims, with jurisdiction over most claims for money damages against the United States, disputes over federal contracts and unlawful "takings" of private property by the federal government. A lower court's ruling on an issue of law may be appealed to the intermediate appellate court. In the federal court systems, these intermediate courts are the United States Courts of Appeal. The 94 federal district courts are organized into **12 regional appellate courts and the US Court of Appeals for the Federal Circuit**. These courts hear appeals from the district courts and federal administrative agencies. The Court of Appeals for the Federal Circuit, located in Washington, has nationwide jurisdiction to hear appeals from specialized cases, like patent cases, as well as appeals for the Court of International Trade and Court of Federal Claims.

Insolvenzgericht
bundesweite Zuständigkeit
internationaler Handel

Schadensersatz in Geld

Privateigentum – Bundesregierung – Entscheidung – Rechtsfrage

4. State Courts

Most cases come before the state courts. Each state by constitution and statute has established its own system, and the lack of uniformity makes it impossible to give a detailed description to fit all states. When the state courts were established travel was difficult. That is the reason why a number of courts of general jurisdiction was created to bring justice close to the people. Recently, considerable progress has been made in the simplification of state court systems and the improvement of judicial administration. In the state trial courts a **single judge presides**, whether there is a jury or not. The judge is generally **authorized to hear all cases, civil and criminal**. At the top of the state judicial system is the highest appellate court of that state. In most states it is called simply the supreme court; in some it is known by another name, such as the court of appeals in New York.

werden verhandelt
einführen
fehlende Übereinstimmung
Vereinfachung
Verbesserung
vorsitzen – Geschworene
zuständig

II. Their Tasks

The courts enforce statutes and interpret them. They also invalidate unconstitutional statutes, and make law in areas not covered by statutes. Here are some examples of the four main roles played by U.S. courts:

Geltung verschaffen – auslegen
für ungültig erklären

1. Enforcement

The Copyright Act gives a copyright owner the exclusive right to reproduce the owner's work. A copyright infringement suit is an example of court **enforcement of a statute**.

Gesetz zum Urheberrecht
Verletzung
Vollstreckung, Geltendmachung

2. Interpretation

According to the Copyright Act, the copyright in a work created by an employee within the scope of his employment is owned by the employer. The Copyright Act does not define the term "employee". The Supreme Court case that defines the term is an example of court **interpretation of a statute**.

Angestellter – Bereich, Rahmen
Auslegung

3. Invalidation

The courts **invalidate unconstitutional laws**. Unconstitutional laws are laws that conflict with provisions of the Constitution. The Constitution is the supreme law of the United States. Many "constitutionality" cases involve claims that a law violates the Constitution's Bill of Rights (the first ten amendments). In Roe v. Wade, the Supreme Court invalidated a state statute restricting women's access to abortion. According to the Court, the statute violated a pregnant woman's constitutional right of privacy (see Infra, page 77).

für ungültig erklären
verfassungswidrig
Grundrechteerklärung
Zusatz
einschränken – Zugang
Abtreibung
schwanger – unten

4. Making Law

The courts **create the law for "common law"** subject areas. Common law covers areas not covered by statutes. In many states, for example, individuals' rights of privacy and publicity are protected under common law rather than under statutory laws.

schaffen

Diagram 2

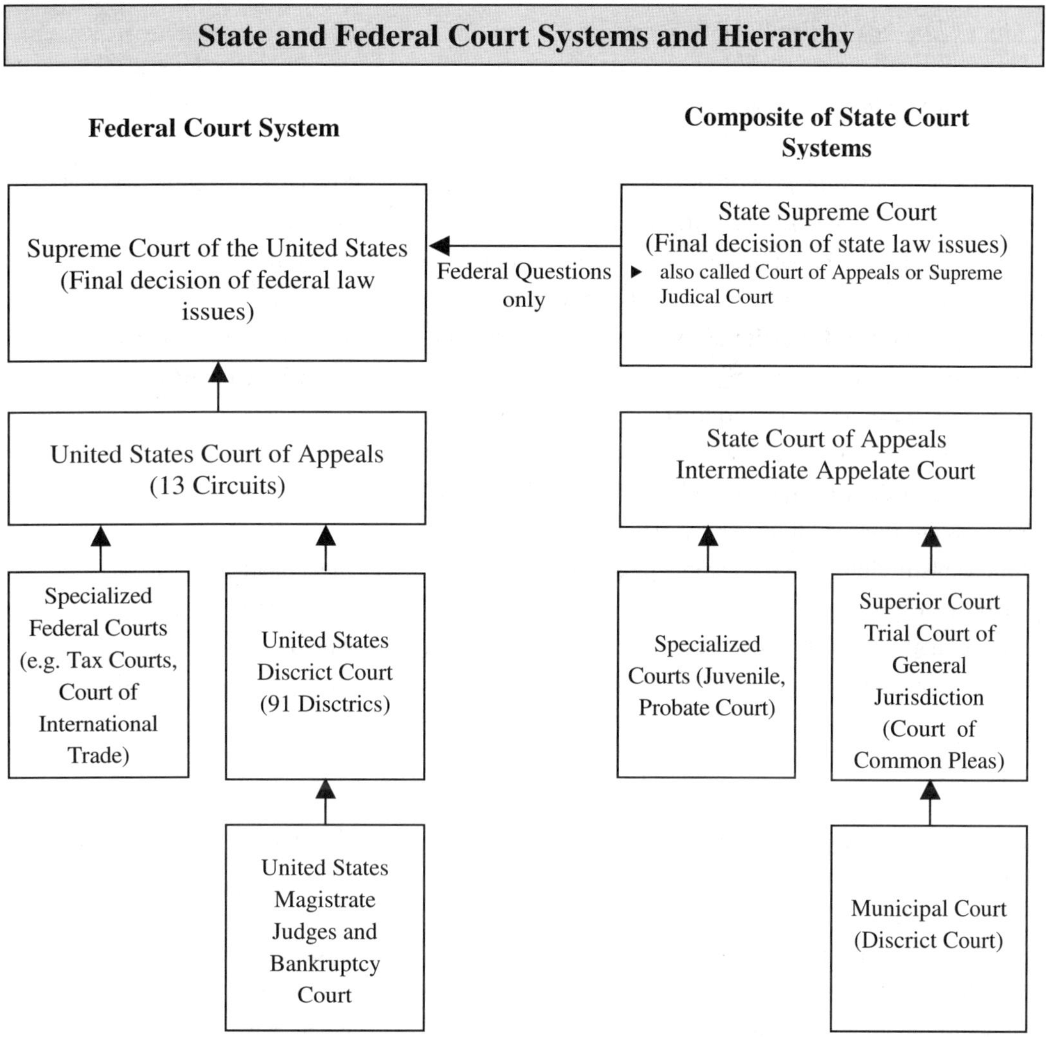
State and Federal Court Systems and Hierarchy
Federal Court System
Composite of State Court Systems
Supreme Court of the United States (Final decision of federal law issues)
Federal Questions only
State Supreme Court (Final decision of state law issues)
▸ also called Court of Appeals or Supreme Judical Court
United States Court of Appeals (13 Circuits)
State Court of Appeals Intermediate Appelate Court
Specialized Federal Courts (e.g. Tax Courts, Court of International Trade)
United States Discrict Court (91 Disctrics)
Specialized Courts (Juvenile, Probate Court)
Superior Court Trial Court of General Jurisdiction (Court of Common Pleas)
United States Magistrate Judges and Bankruptcy Court
Municipal Court (Discrict Court)

B. Legislative Branch

I. Laws Classified by Federal and State

1. Federal Statutes

The U.S. Constitution gives Congress the power to enact federal laws ("statutes") on certain subjects.
The Copyright Act is one example of a statute adopted by Congress. Congress's power to enact the Copyright Act stems from **Article I, Section 8**, of the Constitution, which authorizes Congress to establish laws giving "authors and inventors the exclusive right to their respective writings and discoveries" to encourage progress in the arts and sciences.
According to the Constitution, all powers not delegated to Congress are reserved to the states. The "commerce clause" of the Constitution, which concerns interstate commerce, is generally viewed as giving Congress broad power to regulate matters affecting interstate commerce - trademarks used in interstate commerce, for example.

Macht, Kompetenz – Gesetz erlassen
annehmen
stammen von
ermächtigen – erlassen
Erfinder
übertragen
innerstaatlicher Handel
Marke

2. State Statutes

State legislatures can pass laws on matters for which they **share jurisdiction with Congress**. Trademark law is an example of a shared jurisdiction. In other matters, the federal government has taken exclusive jurisdiction. Copyright is an example: The Copyright Act prohibits the states from granting copyright-like protection.
States can also pass laws on **matters in which the Constitution does not grant jurisdiction to the federal government**.

Staatengesetzgeber – Gesetz erlassen
ausschließlich
verbieten
gewähren

II. How to Make a Law

The U.S. Congress has exclusive authority to enact federal legislation. The process by which a proposed bill becomes a law can be very complex and take years.

Gesetzesvorschlag

1. Introduction of Bills

Bills may originate in either the House of Representatives or the Senate, unless a bill involves raising revenue, in which case it must originate in the House of Representatives.
Only **Senators and Representatives** (also known as Members of Congress) **can introduce a bill** in their respective chamber. When bills are introduced, they are given a bill number. The numbering system starts over with each session of Congress, and bill numbers run in chronological order according to when the bill is introduced. Bills in the House of Representatives are given the initial **H.R.**, and Senate Bills are given the initial **S.** Thus, H.R. 1, would be the first bill introduced in a new session of Congress or the House of Representatives.

herrühren
ist verbunden mit –Staatsein-
nahmen
einbringen
jeweilig
Sitzungsperiode
Anfangsbuchstabe

2. Committee Consideration

After a bill is introduced, it is assigned to one or more committees in the chamber where it was introduced. A **committee can amend, rewrite, recommend, or ignore the bill** or report back to the full chamber with no recommendation. Committees typically also submit a report explaining their views of the bill when sending a bill to the full House or Senate.

übertragen
Kommitee
ergänzen – umschreiben –
empfehlen – ignorieren
zufügen

3. Floor Debate and Vote

Once the bill has emerged from committee consideration, it moves to the **"floor" of either the House of Representatives or the Senate** (again depending on where the bill was introduced). The entire chamber then debates and may amend the bill. The chamber then takes an open vote on the bill. For non-controversial votes, the chamber will take a voice vote, but if any legislator asks for a roll call, then each member's vote is made separately and publicly.

hervorkommen – Beratung
ganz
ergänzen – offen Abstimmung
Abstimmung durch Zuruf –
namentliche Abstimmung

4. Passage in Both Chambers

If the bill passes the first chamber, it is sent to the other chamber where the **process described above is repeated**. If the bill is amended in the second chamber, it must be sent back to the first chamber because both chambers must agree on the amendments. If the two chambers cannot immediately agree on how to pass identical legislation, the bill will be sent to a **joint committee** (comprised of both House of Representatives and Senate members), which will attempt to work out a **compromise** among the different versions of the bill. If the joint committee is successful, the bill will be returned to both chambers for a vote.

durchlaufen
ergänzen
gemeinsames Kommitee
versuchen
Abstimmung

5. Overriding a Presidential Veto

Once an identical bill passes both the House and the Senate, it is sent to the President, who can do the following. He can **sign it**, thus creating a law. If he does **nothing, it becomes law** after 10 days, if Congress stays in session. If he **does nothing** and if Congress adjourns within 10 days, **it does not become law**. Finally, if he **rejects the bill** by vetoing it, the bill will not become law unless the veto is overridden by Congress.
Congress may override the President's veto by approving the bill again with at least a two-thirds majority vote in both the House and the Senate. The bill becomes a law despite the President's veto.

ablehnen
Veto einlegen, untersagen –
überstimmt

Diagram 3

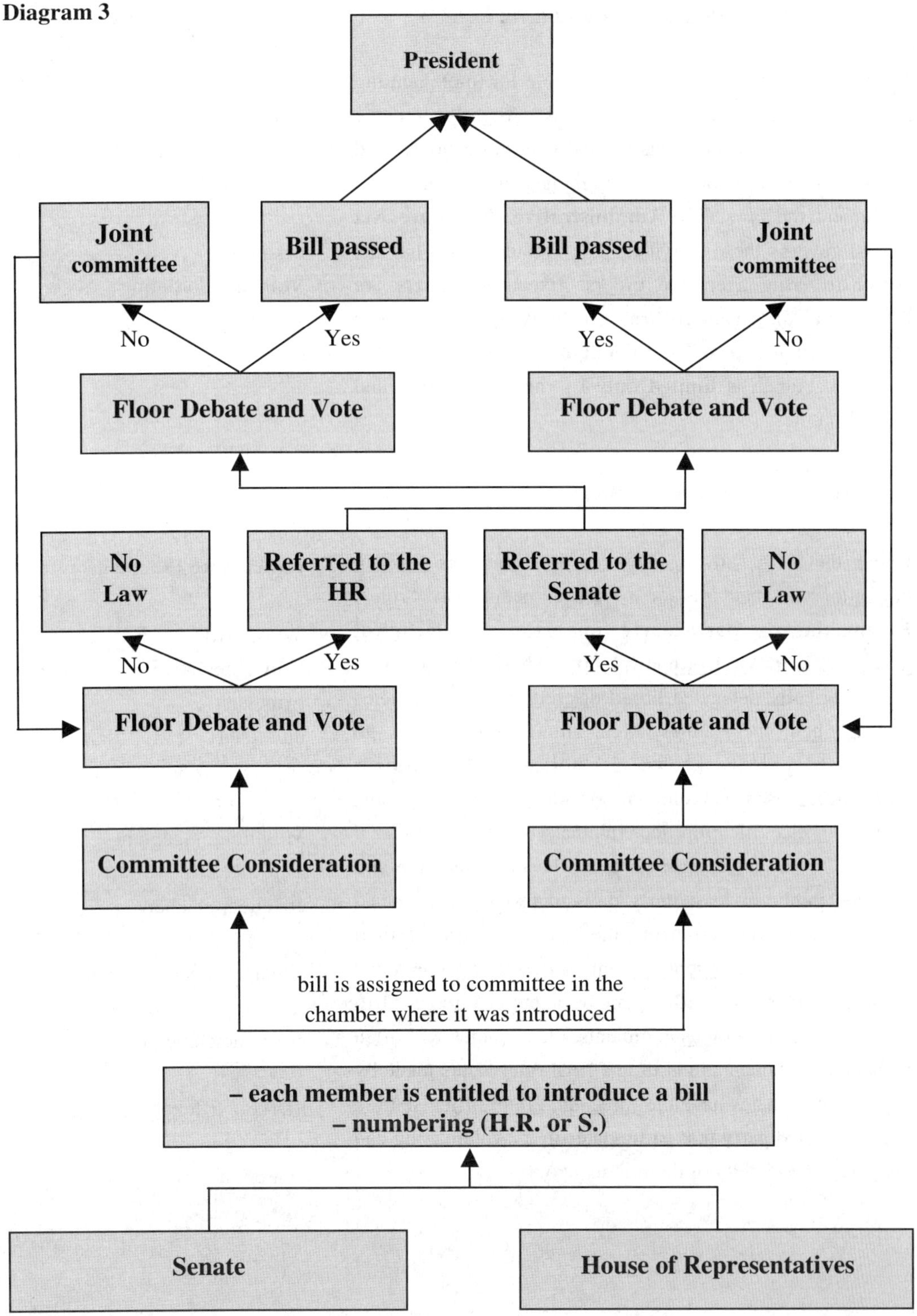
President
Joint committee
Bill passed
Bill passed
Joint committee
No
Yes
Yes
No
Floor Debate and Vote
Floor Debate and Vote
No Law
Referred to the HR
Referred to the Senate
No Law
No
Yes
Yes
No
Floor Debate and Vote
Floor Debate and Vote
Committee Consideration
Committee Consideration
bill is assigned to committee in the chamber where it was introduced
– each member is entitled to introduce a bill
– numbering (H.R. or S.)
Senate
House of Representatives

III. Role of the Executive in the Law-Making Process

The U.S. Executive Branch is responsible for implementing most laws passed by the Congress. Agencies in the executive branch issue rules, make adjudications, and provide other opinions and guidelines in an effort to implement the laws. The **Administrative Procedure Act (APA)** governs these activities. The President also has the power to issue executive orders. Executive orders are Presidential directives governing actions by other federal officials and agencies. The **President's authority** over the executive branch **is limited** only by the Constitution and federal statutes.

umsetzen
Behörden
erlassen – Entscheidung
Richtlinie
bestimmt
Vollzugsanordnung
Anweisung

1. Notice and Comment Rulemaking

Under the APA, any agency decision that sets binding obligations or standards for a class of people is a "rule". **Rulemaking is particularly important in technical areas, such as environmental law**, where the Congress has historically delegated broad discretion to the agencies to implement the statutes. Most administrative rules go through a process known as **notice and comment rulemaking**. Before issuing most rules, the agency must issue a notice of proposed rulemaking in the *Federal Register*. This notice must describe the proposed rule and give the public at least thirty days to provide comments. After receiving the comments, the agency can issue a final rule, along with a general statement describing the rule's authority and purpose. Because the agency is required to consider all nonfrivolous comments, the agencies will often respond to comments in issuing a final rule. Rules made by regulatory agencies have the force and effect of legislation. Any interested party that participates in the rulemaking can challenge the legality of the rule in a court.

verbindliche Pflichten
fachspezifischer Bereich
Umweltrecht
Ermessen
umsetzen
Mitteilung – geplant
erstellen, machen
allgemeine Stellungnahme
ernst zu nehmend
Stärke – Effekt
angreifen

2. Adjudications

The second major type of agency action is an **adjudication**. Adjudications occur where the agency is making a **binding, case-specific decision**, such as siting, permitting, or licensing a particular activity or facility. In such instances, the agencies are acting like courts in making decisions that settle specific disputes between parties or between the government and a party. Under the APA, these adjudications must be made "on the record after opportunity for a hearing". Any party to the adjudication can typically appeal the decision for judicial review.

Entscheidung
entstehen
platzieren
Einrichtung

schlichten – Streitigkeit

Diagram 4

Legislative Branch, Art. 1

The Congress

House of Representatives
(Art. 1 Sec. 2)

- members are chosen every second year
- minimum age: 25 years
- each state has at least one Representative; number shall not exceed one for every 30.000 citizens
- minimum citizenship: 7 years

United States Senate
(Art. 1 Sec. 3)

- 100 members (two of each state)
- senators are elected by the people of the entire state (method of election changed by Amend. XVII)
- 6 years
- minimum age: 35 years
- mimimum citizenship: 9 years

C. Executive Branch

The executive branch includes the **President**, the **Vice President**, the **Cabinet** and all federal departments, and most governmental agencies.

Exekutive

I. The President

All executive power of the government is vested in the President, who serves a **four-year term**, U.S. Const. art. II, sec. 1, cl. 1 and can be reelected once.. The President is the **Commander in Chief** of the military, U.S. Const. art. II, sec. 2, cl. 1, and has primary authority over foreign affairs. The President has the **power to make treaties**, but only with the approval of two-thirds of the U.S. Senate, U.S. Const. art. II, sec. 2, cl. 2. The President also has the power to **nominate all Supreme Court Justices**, all other federal judges, ambassadors, and all other officers of the United States. U.S. Const. art. II, sec. 2, cl. 2. The President has the power to **veto legislation**.

im Amt sein
primär
Außenpolitik
Vertrag
Zustimmung
nominieren
Botschafter
Veto erheben

II. The Vice President

The Vice President is also the **President of the Senate**, but votes only in the case of a tie vote in the Senate, U.S. Const. art. I, sec. 3, cl. 4. The Vice President serves the same four-year term as the President, U.S. Const. art. II, sec. 1, cl. 1.

Pattsituation

III. Government Departments

The President selects the heads of the **14 government departments**. These departments are **not specified in the Constitution** and have varied in name and number over time. They now are the Departments of State, Treasury, Defense, Justice, Interior, Agriculture, Commerce, Labor, Health and Human Services, Housing and Urban Development, Transportation, Energy, Education, and Veterans Affairs. The heads of the departments form the Cabinet, which is the highest advisory group to the

auswählen
veränderlich sein
Außenministerium – Finanzmin. – Verteidigungsmin. – Innenmin. – Handelsmin. – Arbeitsmin. – Stadt- und Wohnungsmin. – Ministerium für Veteranen – Beratungsgremium

President. The executive branch also includes dozens of **government agencies**. The primary difference between agencies and departments is that agencies <u>serve</u> a very specific need.

dienen

<u>IV. Government Offices and Agencies</u>

Government offices and agencies play an important role in the legal system. The **Copyright Office** and the **U.S. Patent and Trademark Office** are the key federal government offices for multimedia developers and publishers.

Diagram 5

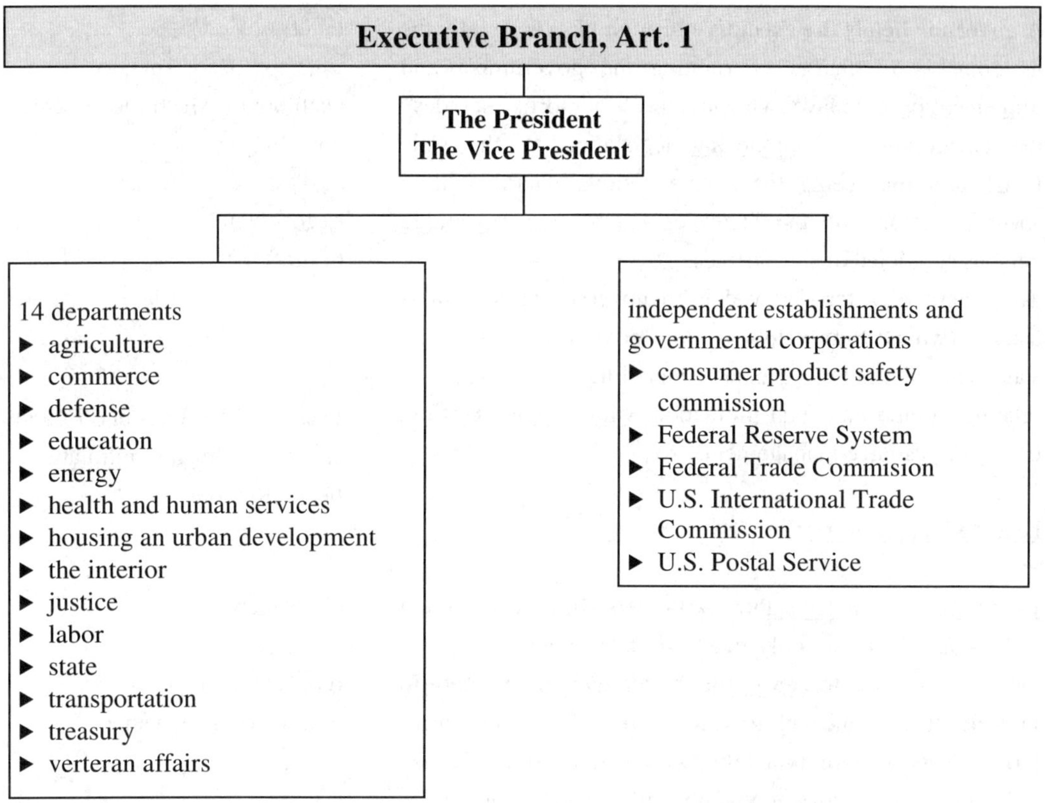

Part 4: Subnational Governments

Each of the fifty states in the U.S. share certain characteristics: each government is **based on a written constitution**, which cannot contradict the federal constitution; each has a **republican form of government** comprised of the same three branches (executive, legislative and judicial) as the federal government and containing a similar **system of checks and balances**, and **separation of powers**. Within these broad similarities, however, there can be significant differences in governmental structures among the various states.

teilen
widersprechen
zusammensetzen
starke Ähnlichkeiten
erheblich

A. The Governor

A governor heads the executive branch of every state; the governor is in charge of running the government and implementing state laws. The governor's authority includes the developing and proposing legislation to the state legislature, overseeing the state's national guard, calling special sessions of the state legislature and pardoning persons convicted of state crimes.
The length of a term served by a governor varies but is usually **two or four years**. A state governor oversees the state administrative agencies, including those agencies relating to environmental protection, wildlife conservation, or natural resource management.

leitet
ausführen – Macht, Kompetenz
vorschlagen
begnadigen
bestraft
Erhaltung der Tier- und Pflanzenwelt – Umgang mit natürlichen Ressourcen

B. State Legislatures

Every state has a legislature with **two chambers**, except Nebraska, which has only one. All state legislatures serve the same purpose: to **represent the citizens of the state in making laws concerning state issues**. State legislative terms vary, but are typically two or four years. Unlike federal laws, state laws only apply within a state's borders.

Gesetzgeber
repräsentieren
einzelstaatenbezogene Fragen
Grenze

C. State Judiciaries

All state judiciaries are **hierarchical**, like the federal system. State systems are made up of a Supreme Court (sometimes with a different name), usually an **intermediate appellate court**, and a **series of lower courts** or trial courts, sometimes including specialized courts. State judiciaries interpret state laws and apply them in specific disputes relating to state law; they determine whether a state crime has been committed; they evaluate the constitutionality of state laws under the state constitution; and they review the legality of state administrative rules under state statutes.

hierarchisch
mittlerer
Berufungsgericht
feststellen
begehen – Verfassungsgemäßheit

D. Local Government

Local governments, unlike state governments or the federal government, are not **directly defined by a constitution** though many state constitutions determine the process for creating a local government. For example, although many state constitutions determine the process for creating a local government, in many states, the state legislature must vote on the charter for any local government structure. Local government structures may vary, but they typically include counties, cities, villages, and townships. **City governments most commonly include an elected mayor, which is the chief executive**, and a city council, which acts much like a legislature. Villages and townships are often found in more rural areas; they may have a structure similar to that of a city or be run by a commission. Most states are divided into counties, usually with an elected board of county commissioners or supervisors. There may also be other elected county officials, including **sheriffs or county executives**. In addition, many special purpose delegates carry out such functions as education and sometimes environmental regulation.

Local governments, including cities and counties, often have **important environmental responsibilities**, such as managing solid waste, ensuring clean drinking water, developing and enforcing land-use plans, inspecting local

Kommunale Regierung
abstimmen
Schaffung
Kreis – Stadt – Dorf – Ortschaft – Bürgermeister
Kommunale Spitze
ländliche Gegend
Kommission
Aufsichtspersonen
Erziehung
Umwelt
(fester) Abfall – absichern
baurechtliche Pläne

restaurants and other establishments for health and safety, and providing emergency services and planning. More generally, local governments have the power to tax, to enact and enforce local ordinances, and to administer the local aspects of certain state and federal programs.

Notdienst
Steuerhebungsrecht
Satzung

Part 5: Sources and Hierarchy of Law

A. The Constitution

The Constitution of the United States is the **"supreme law of the land;"** it provides the basis for the U.S. government, and guarantees the freedom and rights of all U.S. citizens. No laws may contradict any of the Constitution's principles and no governmental authority in the U.S. is exempt from complying with it. The federal courts have the sole authority to interpret the Constitution and to evaluate the federal constitutionality of federal or state laws.

ausgeschlossen
entsprechen
auslegen – bewerten
Verfassungsmäßigkeit

B. International Treaties

Treaties entered into by the United States are also considered the **supreme law of the land pursuant to the U.S. Constitution**, as are federal laws. In the case of a conflict between a treaty and a federal statute, the one that is later in time or more specific will typically control. Treaties to which the United States is a party may be found in the U.S. Treaties Service, the Statutes at Large, the Treaties and other International Acts Series issued by the State Department, as well as the United Nations Treaty Series.

Vertrag
Bundesgesetz
regelmäßig Vorrang haben
herausgeben – Außenministerium

C. Federal Statutes

Federal Statutes are published first in Slip Law, then in the Statutes at Large, and subsequently in the **United States Code**. An example of a cite to a federal statute is: 42 U.S.C. sec. 9607, which would refer to title 42, section 9607 of the U.S. Code. **Federal statutes may be challenged in federal court.**

zitieren
angreifen; infrage stellen

D. Agency Rules and Executive Orders

Federal administrative bodies issue rules and regulations of a **quasi-legislative character**; valid federal regulations have the force of law and preempt state laws and rules. Rules and regulations may be issued only under statutory authority granted by Congress. The President also has broad powers to issue executive orders. An **executive order is a directive from the President to other officials in the executive branch**. Proposed and final rules, executive orders, and other executive branch notices are published daily in the Federal Register.

Gesetzeskraft – vorgehen
gewähren – weitreichende Gewalt

Every federal agency must publish:

- descriptions of its **organizational structure**;
- general statements of how the **agency functions**;
- its **rules of procedures**, available forms and descriptions of all papers, final reports or examinations;
- and, all substantive rules or **statements of general applicability** adopted by the agency. Rules may be challenged in federal court. The federal courts have sole authority to review agency rules and actions to ensure that they are legal under the substantive federal statute.

veröffentlichen
Organisationsstruktur
Verfahrensregeln
materielle Regeln
Anwendbarkeit – erlassen

E. Judicial Opinions

The United States is a common law country. Every U.S. state has a legal system based on the **common law**, except Louisiana (which relies on the French civil code). Common law has **no statutory basis**; judges establish common law by applying previous decisions **(precedents)** to present cases. Although typically affected by statutory authority, broad areas of the law, most notably relating to property, contracts, and torts are traditionally part of the common law. These areas of the law are mostly within the jurisdiction of the states, and thus **state courts are the primary source of common law**. Federal common law is relatively narrow in scope, being limited primarily to clearly federal issues that have not been addressed by a statute.

basieren
Gesetzesgrundlage – erlassen
frühere Entscheidung
Sachenrecht
Vertragsrecht – Deliktsrecht
Zuständigkeit
primäre Quelle

Reported decisions of the U.S. Supreme Court and of most of the state appellate courts can be found in the official reporter of the respective courts. Those decided from at least 1887 to date can also be found in the **National Reporter System**, a system of unofficial reporters. Decisions of lower state courts are not published officially, but can usually be found in unofficial reports. When referring to a case, a citation typically includes the name of the case and the volume and pages of the reporter, as well as the date.

Veröffentlichte Entscheidungen – offizielle Entscheidungssammlung – jeweilig

nicht offiziell

sich beziehen auf

Diagram 6

Name ot the Case	Volume of the Reporter	Name of the Reporter	Page of the Reporter	Year of Dicision
Martin v. Hunter's Lessee	14	U.S.	304	1816
Hamer v. Sidway	27	N.E.	256	1891
United States v. Braunstein	75	F. Supp.	137	1947
Rhen Marshall, Inc. .v Purolator Filter Div.	318	N.W. 2d	284	1982

List of Important Reporters' Names		
▶ U.S.	=	United States Supreme Court Reports
▶ N.E.	=	North Eastern Reporter
▶ F. Supp.	=	Federal Supplement
▶ N.W. 2d	=	North Western Reporter, Second Series
▶ F	=	Federal Reporter
▶ F.2d	=	Federal Reporter, Second Series

F. State Constitutions and Statutes

State constitutions are the supreme law within the state. State statutes must conform to the respective state's constitution. All state constitutions and legislation can be preempted by federal legislation or the federal Constitution.

höchstes Recht

übereinstimmen

Part 6: Finding the Law

Law is made by the courts on a precedent basis following the doctrine of stare decisis. Furthermore, it is also made by Congress and the state legislatures. Knowing the law on a given topic generally requires a review of both statutory law and case law.	"starre Entscheidung" Gebiet – Überprüfung – Gesetzesrecht – Fallrecht

A. Statutes

Federal and state statutory laws can be found by consulting published **"codifications"** of laws in law libraries maintained by law schools, law firms, courts, and bar associations. To find a federal law such as the Copyright Act, for example, one would look in the **United States Code**, which is divided into **"titles"**. Federal and state statutory laws can also be obtained "on-line" from **Westlaw** or **Lexis**, two computerized legal research services.	unterhalten – Vereinigung der Juristen in Amerika

B. Court Decisions

Court decisions (also known as "case law") can be found in publications called **"reporters"**. For example, decisions of the United States Supreme Court are published in the United States Reports, the Supreme Court Reporter, and the Lawyers Edition (three different "reporters" from three different publishers).	Veröffentlichung
These decisions are also available from computerized services such as Westlaw and Lexis, which provide on-line research assistance for **locating cases on desired topics**. "Digests" that divide decided cases into topics are also helpful for locating relevant cases. Other research resources help lawyers determine whether cases in which they are interested have been reversed by a higher court or overruled (modified by a later decision of the same court).	Recherchehilfe Auszug, Übersicht Recherchequelle aufheben
Various publishing companies publish **"annotated" statutory** codes, which bring statutes and relevant court decisions together in one source. West Publishing Company, for example, publishes the **United States Code Annotated**, which lists the court decisions enforcing or interpreting each provision of the United States Code.	Verleger

Diagram 7

Sources and Hierarchy of Law

Constitution

International Treaties, Art. 2, sec. 2

Federal Statues, examples
- Lanham Act
- Patent Law

Agency Rules and Executive Orders
- issued by federal administrations or the President
- must be published

Judical opinions
- system of precedents

State Constitution
and Statutes

Part 7: The Legal Profession

A. Introduction

The American lawyer is fortunate in the wide range of activities in which he may engage and in the ease with which he may move from one branch of the profession to another.	glücklich Bequemlichkeit, Leichtigkeit

B. Judges

I. Characteristics of Judges

Virtually all judges today are **members of the bar**. As such they have gone through the same legal education and procedures for acceptance into the bar as every attorney in the U.S. At one point in United States history, judges were	So gut wie juristische Ausbildung Anwalt

neither members of the bar nor even trained in law. From colonial times until well into the nineteenth century, **"lay judges"** were not uncommon in the United States. Things are different today, although there are still a few non-lawyer judges in some rural areas in some states.

Laienrichter – ungewöhnlich

Judges in the United States almost always come to the bench following several years of law practice, whether as private lawyers, prosecutors, or public defenders. Because of this, new judges in the United States tend to be older than their counterparts in civil law countries, most of whom start out on the judicial ladder shortly after finishing their legal education. Part of the Anglo-American tradition of preferring older judges has to do with **the need for the judge to have gained adequate knowledge of the law and the complexities of court procedure**, particularly how to handle the relatively complicated trial process for which law school does not prepare them particularly well. But it is more than that. **Experience**, not just as a lawyer, but **in life**, is deemed essential for the exercise of mature judgement, which many view as the hallmark of a good judge in the United States. This is particularly so in a common-law system where **judges have law-making capacities**.

Richterposten – juristische (Berufs-) Praxis – Staatsanwalt – (öffentlicher) Verteidiger
Gegenstück
erlangen
erstinstanzliche Verfahren
angesehen, erachtet – reife Entscheidung – Merkmal
Möglichkeit

II. Career Paths of Judges

Career paths of judges in the United States differ from the career paths of judges in civil law countries. Judges in the United States usually do not start at the bottom of the judicial ladder and work their way up to positions on higher courts and more responsibility. A judge in the United States who starts out at the trial level is likely to remain there unless he makes some effort to gain the attention of the electorate or political appointing authorities. There is **no official "performance review" system**. Similarly, a judge can start a judicial career at any level in the judiciary, depending on his ability to influence the voters or the inclinations of the appointing authorities. Thus, a lawyer who has no prior judicial experience can become a justice on a court of last resort in a state or even the United States Supreme Court. This was the case with one of the more

Karrierewege
Verantwortlichkeit
bleiben
Wähler – politische Ernennungseinrichtung
Fähigkeit – Wähler
(Zu-) Neigung

distinguished justices of the Court, Felix Frankfurter, who came to the Court after a 25-year law-teaching career.

ausgezeichnet

In fact, fewer than half of the justices who have served on the United States Supreme Court had prior judicial experience of any kind. Six of the eleven Reagan and Bush appointees to the **District of Columbia Court of Appeals**, which is perhaps the most influential of the federal circuit courts of appeal, had no prior judicial experience. Four were law professors, one was a former member of Congress, and one was a lawyer for the Department of Justice. Interestingly enough, there is no legal requirement that federal judges even be lawyers or have a law degree.

Ernannte
einflussreich
gerichtliche Erfahrung
Justizministerium
Jura-Abschluss

III. Judges as Political Beings

As will be discussed shortly, under most judicial selection systems in the United States, **judges either run for election by the general population or are appointed by elected officials**. Consequently, becoming either a federal or state judge depends in large part on the would-be judge's ability to attract political support. It is not surprising then to find out that many **judges in the United States are "political" people** – persons who have been involved in politics on a regular basis in some capacity, whether as office holders, such as legislators or executive officials, or as political organizers, campaign managers or party chairmen. It is sometimes the case, especially for judicial candidates for appellate courts, that any law practice experience they had ended many years ago and was superseded by a much longer political career. Whatever their past political background, however, once on the bench, judges are not supposed to engage in partisan political activity.

richterliches Auswahlsystem
Bevölkerung – ernennen
politische Unterstützung bekommen
Wahlkampforganisator – Parteivorsitzender
ersetzen, ablösen
Richterstuhl
parteiisch, kämpferisch

But while a judge may have to cease political activity of the partisan sort after going on the bench, the political orientation of candidates continues to make itself felt after appointment through their "judicial philosophy" – attitudes about the role of courts in society. That philosophy might be a **"liberal-activist"** one that emphasizes the role of courts in fighting social injustice and expanding individual rights, or it may focus on a more **"conservative"** judicial restraint,

Einstellung
betonen
soziale Ungerechtigkeit
Beschränkung

which maintains that courts should rarely intervene to upset a legislative judgement or interfere with administrative action. More recently, a "conservative activist" philosophy has emerged on the Supreme Court among conservative appointees who have sought to upset liberal precedents.	einschreiten sich einmischen Ernannte – umwerfen – Vorgänger
A judge's political viewpoint is likely to have some effect on such "non-political" issues as the proper limits of tort recovery for personal injury, the rights of consumers against manufacturers, the rights of criminal defendants or even the rights of shareholders in a corporation against management. More generally, **all people – including judges – tend naturally to be inclined one way or the other in disputes between governments and individuals**, between governments and businesses, between rich and poor, between businesses and individuals, or even between state and federal governments. This is not to say that judicial decisions can be made on overtly political grounds. However, when deciding close questions between two different lines of authority – where a rational choice supported by caselaw or statute could be made either way – political views can have a strong influence.	Anspruch aus Delikt Verbraucherrechte Hersteller – strafrechtlich Verfolgter – Aktionär – Unternehmen geneigt sein offen
It should be emphasized that political attitudes of the type discussed are so basic that they are often unconscious or, when conscious, are not thought of as being political. Those attitudes are in any event no different from the kinds of attitudes that often influence judicial decision-making in other legal systems. But the fact that judges in the United States have a well-developed political "past" makes the connection of attitude to decision more transparent. It is not uncommon for lawyers in an important case to **read the judicial opinions and research the political background of the judge before whom they are soon to appear** for some insight into the judge's basic political attitudes, so that they may better frame their arguments and assess their chances of success.	unbewusst Beziehung – Einstellung – Entscheidung Einblick formulieren – festlegen
Judicial philosophy and political attitudes of a judge can grow and change, especially with the judicial independence guaranteed by lifetime tenure in the federal system and some state systems. For example, United States Supreme Court justices have produced surprises for Presidents who	lebenslange Amtszeit

nominated them. The most notable of these was Earl Warren, a former Republican governor of California who was appointed by Republican President Dwight D. Eisenhower as Chief Justice. Following his appointment, the Warren Court proceeded to issue liberal opinions on civil rights, rights of the accused in criminal cases and in other areas, much to the dismay of conservatives. This led the war hero President Eisenhower to remark later that his **appointment of Earl Warren was the "worst damn-fool mistake I ever made as President"**. Both William Brennan, appointed by Eisenhower, and Harry A. Blackmun, appointed by Republican President Richard M. Nixon, were Republicans who turned liberal on the Court. On the other side, Justice Byron White, appointed by Democrat John F. Kennedy, was a disappointment to liberals as he often sided with the conservative faction of the Supreme Court in criminal procedure and other cases involving constitutional rights of the individual.

ernennen
fortfahren
Beschuldigter
Bestürzung
liberal werden
Enttäuschung

C. Attorneys

Depending upon the circumstances and the needs of the client, the lawyer may be

- a **counselor**,
- a **negotiator**, and/or
- a **litigator**.

In each of these roles, the lawyer will need to engage in factual investigation. With the respect to each of these roles, the lawyer will do the following:

Untersuchung

I. Counselor

Attorney will help **advise the client how to order the client's affairs**, how or whether to proceed with a proposed course of action, or how to proceed with respect to pending or potential litigation or settlement. Often, this is when the lawyer will prepare an interoffice memorandum of law, which will examine the client's legal position and help the lawyer counsel the client.

beraten
gegenwärtig
mögliches Verfahren – Einigung – internes Schriftstück

II. Negotiator

The lawyer will work with opposing counsel to **try to get a favorable resolution for the client with respect to a pending dispute**. The parties may already be in litigation when they negotiate, or the parties, through their attorneys, may be negotiating a resolution to a dispute not yet in court. The art of negotiation involves many techniques individual to particular attorneys and the circumstances. The client always retains the right to accept or reject a settlement negotiated or offered by the opposing party.

gegnerischer Anwalt
günstige
Streitigkeit

annehmen – ablehnen

III. Litigator

In litigation, the attorney will **help pick a jury and participate in pre-trial motions**. At trial, the attorney will present evidence through testimony of witnesses, documents and perhaps demonstrative evidence. The lawyer will also present an opening statement and closing argument, and will make and respond to evidentiary objections lodged by the opposing party. The lawyer may also make motions, sometimes supported by a memorandum in support thereof before the court, and propose to the court a set of jury instructions.

Geschworene
vorgerichtlich
Zeuge
Augenscheinsbeweis
Eröffnungsrede – Plädoyer
Einwände die Beweis betreffend

Anweisungen an die Geschworenen

Further reading

Literatur zur Vertiefung

Crump, Cases and Materials on Constitutional Law, 3rd ed., 1998; *Redlich/Attanasio/Goldstein,* Constitutional Law, 4th ed., 2001; *Barron/Dienes/McCormick,* Constitutional Law: Principles and Policy, 5th ed., 1995; *Braveman/Banks/Smolla,* Constitutional Law: Structure and Rights in Our Federal System, 4th ed., 2000; *Nowak/Rotunda,* Handbook on Constitutional Law, 4th ed., 1991; *Tribe*, American Constitutional Law, 2nd ed., 1988; *Wechsler,* Principles, Politics and Fundamental Law, 1961; *Ely,* Democracy and Distrust: A Theory on Judicial Review, 1980; *Sunstein,* The Partial Constitution, 1993; *Marks/Cooper,* State Constitutional Law in a Nutshell, 1988.

Chapter Two

Constitutional Law

Part 1: Introduction

The US Constitution has a great impact on the US law. On the one hand it deals with the powers of the three branches: legislative, executive, judicial. On the other hand one can find especially in the Amendments the rights of a US citizen. In this chapter, the following aspects will be reviewed:

Einfluss

Verfassungszusätze

- **Supreme Court's authority (part 2)**: What did the court say in *Marbury v. Madison*? What is standing, ripeness and mootness? Are there limitations on exercise of federal jurisdiction?
- **federalism and federal power (part 3):** What is the Commerce Clause? How did the Supreme Court decide in *Lopez*? What entails the necessary and proper clause? What do we mean talking about the system of enumerated powers?
- **executive power (part 4)**: What kind of powers does the President have? What is an executive order?
- **due process of law (part 5)**: Where is the difference between substantial and procedural due process? What is strict scrutiny? Where does the right of privacy come from? Does a woman have a right to terminate her pregnancy by abortion?
- **equal protection (part 6)**: Is it constitutional to differentiate on the basis of race? What did the Supreme Court decide in *Brown v. Board of Education*?
- **freedom of expression (part 7)**: Is it allowed to burn the American flag? What are "fighting words"? What is a content neutral regulation? What is commercial speech?
- **freedom of religion (part 8)**: Where is the difference between the free exercise and the free establishment clause? Is it constitutional to have a mandatory morning prayer in public schools?

Zuständigkeit, Machtbefugnis

Bundesgerichtsbarkeit

zur Folge haben

aufgezählte Befugnisse des Congress

Abtreibung

Gleichbehandlungsgrundsatz

Meinungsäußerungsfreiheit

Ein-, Errichtung

zwingend

The cases cited or discussed here represent only a small portion of the case law that deals with these topics. The discussion is necessarily a <u>cursory</u> one but these issues seem to play a decisive role in constitutional and real life in the U.S.

überblicksartig

Diagram 8

Powers of Three Branches

Congress, Art. 1	**President, Art. 2**	**Judiciary, Art. 3**
▸ Interstate Commerce ▸ Taxing and Spending ▸ Regulating the D.C. ▸ Federal Property ▸ War and Defense ▸ Enforcement of Civil War Amandments	▸ Executions of laws ▸ Commander in Chief ▸ Treaty and Foreign Affairs ▸ Appointment of Federal Officers ▸ Pardons ▸ Veto	▸ cases and controversies that fall within the federal judicial power

Part 2: Judicial Power

As shown in chapter 1 (supra, page 7) the Supreme Court of the United States plays a significant role in constitutional life. The Constitution describes the function and the power of the Court in Article III.

First of all, one should take a look at the Supreme Court's <u>jurisdiction</u>. Regarding the Supreme Court it can be distinguished between original and <u>appellate</u> jurisdiction:

Gerichtsbarkeit
Berufungs-

- Under Article III, Section 2, the Supreme Court has **original jurisdiction** "in all cases affecting <u>Ambassadors</u>, other public Ministers and Consuls, and those in which the State shall be a Party". Therefore, Congress may neither <u>restrict</u> nor enlarge the Supreme Court's original jurisdiction. These cases are very rare.

Zuständigkeit in 1. Instanz
Botschafter
einschränken

► Article III, Section 2, further provides that the Supreme Court shall have **appellate jurisdiction**. Congress has provided two methods for invoking Supreme Court appellate jurisdiction: **appeal** (where jurisdiction is mandatory) and **certiorari** (where it is within the Court's discretion).

Berufungsinstanz
zwingend
Ermessen

A. Review Acts of Legislature

First of all the Supreme Court may review acts of the legislature.

I. Marbury v. Madison

Marbury v. Madison is one of the first cases according to which it is the Supreme Court, not Congress, which has the authority and duty to declare a congressional statute unconstitutional if the Court thinks it violates the Constitution.

verfassungswidrig

Marbury v. Madison, 5 U.S. 137 (1803)

The case began on March 2, 1801, when the Federalist, William Marbury, was designated as a justice of the peace in the District of Columbia. Marbury and several others were appointed to government posts created by Congress in the last days of John Adams's presidency, but these last-minute appointments were never fully finalized. The disgruntled appointees invoked an act of Congress and sued for their jobs in the Supreme Court.

bestimmen, nominieren
Präsidentschaft
verärgert
klagen

Issues
Is Marbury entitled to his appointment? Is his lawsuit the correct way to get it? And, is the Supreme Court the place for Marbury to get the relief he requests?

Streitfrage, strittiger Punkt

Holding and Reasoning

Entscheidung und Begründung

John Marshall (1755–1835)
Chief Justice: 1801–1835
Party: Federalist
Nominated by: J. Adams

Yes. Marshall stated that Marbury had a right to his commission once it was signed. Further, Section 13 of the Judiciary Act of 1789 gave the Supreme Court the right to issue a writ of mandamus against persons holding office. Thus, it would appear that Marbury has a remedy. However, Article III Section 2 of the Constitution states that the Supreme Court shall have original jurisdiction in cases "affecting Ambassadors, other public Ministers and Consuls, and those in which a State shall be a party", and "in all other cases,...shall have appellate jurisdiction". Since a writ of mandamus is an original action, Section 13 of the Judiciary Act must be contrary to the constitution, because it allows the Supreme Court to hear cases of original jurisdiction for persons besides ministers, consuls and ambassadors, etc. If the Constitution is the supreme will of the people to limit government, then the legislature cannot alter it at will. Thus, the legislature cannot be allowed to pass laws repugnant to the constitution. Since it is the Supreme Court's role to interpret laws and resolve conflicts between competing laws, and the Constitution is the supreme law of the land, then the Supreme Court has the power to interpret the Constitution and decide if a law passed conflicts with it.

gerichtliche Verfügung zur Vornahme einer Handlung

im Widerspruch stehen

auslegen

II. Actions of State Governments

In *Martin v. Hunter's Lessee* (see infra, page 36) the Supreme Court went further. It ruled that it had the jurisdiction and authority to review all state acts under the Constitution, laws and treaties of the United States. Justice *Story* found that the Judiciary Act properly recognized the existence of appellate jurisdiction in the Supreme Court over actions in state courts. The **supremacy clause of Article VI** plainly indicates that the framers realized that federal issues might arise in state cases, and the grant of jurisdiction to the Supreme Court in Article III of *all* cases within the judicial power of the United States had to include such decisions.

entscheiden

Gesetz, Vertrag

Verfassungsväter

B. Review Acts of Judiciary

Furthermore, the Supreme Court may also review **acts of the judiciary**. Here one has to distinguish between **state court and federal court** decisions.

I. State Court Decisions

The Supreme Court may review state court opinions, but only to the extent that the decision was decided based on federal law.

überprüfen – Entscheidung
zu dem Ausmaß

Even if there is a federal question in the state court case, the Supreme Court may not review the case if there is an **"independent and adequate" state ground** for the state court's decision. That is, if the same result would be reached even had the state court made a different decision on the federal question, the Supreme Court may not decide the case. This is because its opinion would in effect be an "advisory" one.

Bundes-

beratend, gutachtlich

1. Violations of State and Federal Constitutions

If a state action violates the same clause of both state and federal constitutions, the state court decision may or may not be based on an "independent" state ground. If the state court is saying, "This state action would violate our state constitution whether or not it violated the federal constitution", that is "independent". But if the state court is saying, "Based on our reading of the constitutional provision, this state action violates both constitutions", this is not "independent", so the Supreme Court may review the state court decision.

verletzen

2. Review Limited to Decisions of Highest State Court

Federal statutes limit Supreme Court review to decisions of the highest state court available. But this does not mean that the top-ranking state court must have ruled on the merits of the case in order for the Supreme Court to review it. All that is required is that the case be heard by the highest state court available to the petitioner.

zur Verfügung stehen
nach materiellem Recht

Martin v. Hunter's Lessee – 14 U.S. 304 (1816)

Lord Fairfax held land in Virginia. He was a Loyalist and fled to England during the Revolution. He died in 1781 and left the land to his nephew, Denny Martin, who was a British subject. The following year, the Virginia legislature voided the original land grant and transferred the land back to Virginia. Virginia granted a portion of this land to David Hunter. The Jay Treaty seemed to make clear that Lord Fairfax was entitled to the property. The Supreme Court declared that Fairfax was so entitled, but the Virginia courts, where the suit arose, refused to follow the Supreme Court's decision.

Issue
Does the appellate power of the Supreme Court extend to the Virginia courts?

Holding and Reasoning
Yes. Justice W. Story wrote the opinion of the Supreme Court. In Article III, the Supreme Court is given the judicial power which "shall extend to all cases". Thus, it is the nature of the case and not the court of origin that determines whether the Supreme Court has appellate jurisdiction. The Supreme Court appellate power is not limited only to cases that come up through the lower federal courts. Also, the Constitution was designed to operate upon the states themselves, and not just the persons within the states. Thus, the states themselves are not equal sovereigns with the federal government, but rather subject to its law-making capability. Furthermore, even if the state courts do not abuse the power of the constitution, they are likely to rule differently on it from state to state. Thus, the need for uniformity in decisions requires an ultimate single court of last resort which exercises review over all states. Lastly, there is substantial historical evidence that the framers intended Supreme Court review of state court decisions, as well as several previous cases which do so.

besaß ein Grundstück

Neffe

Staatsbürger

Gesetzgeber – für nichtig erklären

berechtigt

festlegen

gemacht

Souverän

missbrauchen

Einheitlichkeit

Beweis – Verfassungsväter

As a matter of legal history it is not difficult to justify U.S. Supreme Court's review of state court decisions on issues of federal law. During the Constitutional Convention proponents of a strong central government argued that an extensive system of lower courts was necessary to protect federal interests. Proponents of state's rights argued that federal interests were adequately protected by the possibility of review by the Supreme Court. The *Federalist Papers* confirm this understanding, and the first judiciary act, the *Judiciary Act* of 1789, expressly provided for such a review.

Rechtsgeschichte

Verfassungsgebende Versammlung

Befürworter

II. Federal Court Decisions

Article III, Section 2 sets out the **federal judicial power**. This includes, among other things:

- cases arising under the **Constitution** or the "laws of the U.S". (i.e., cases posing a "federal question");
- cases of **admiralty**;
- cases between **two or more states**;
- cases **between citizens of different states**; and
- cases between a state or its citizens and a **foreign country** or foreign citizen.

Bürger

Congress has the general power to decide what types of cases the Supreme Court may hear, so long as it does not expand the Supreme Court's jurisdiction beyond the federal judicial power.

Ex parte Mc Cardle, 74 U.S. 506 (1869)

auf Antrag

McCardle was a newspaper publisher in the post-civil war south. He was imprisoned for sedition. McCardle brought a habeas corpus act under an Act of Congress of 1867 which authorized the federal courts to grant habeas corpus to anyone restrained "in violation of the Constitution", and gave the Supreme Court appellate jurisdiction over such actions. However, before it was

Volksverhetzung

zurückhalten, beschränken

ruled upon on the merits by the Supreme Court, Congress passed another Act, expressly revoking the appellate jurisdiction for these types of actions that it had previously granted in 1867.

zurücknehmen

Issue

Whether Congress can take away the jurisdiction of the Supreme Court as to habeas corpus acts, which jurisdiction was granted in the 1867 Act?

Holding and Reasoning

Yes. It is true that the appellate jurisdiction is granted by the constitution, but in the same article, it is made expressly subject to "such exceptions and under such regulations as Congress shall make". Thus, Congress has the power to expand and limit the scope of the appellate jurisdiction of the Supreme Court. Quite simply, Congress was acting clearly within its power in both granting and then repealing the specific jurisdiction to review habeas corpus cases from the Circuit Courts pursuant to the Act of 1867. The Act of 1868 does not affect the appellate jurisdiction with regard to any other cases.

erweitern – Reichweite

abschaffen, aufheben

Congress also may decide what lower federal courts there should be, and what cases they may hear. Again, the outer bound of this power is that Congress cannot allow the federal courts to hear a case that is not within the federal judicial power.

Außengrenzen

Diagram 9

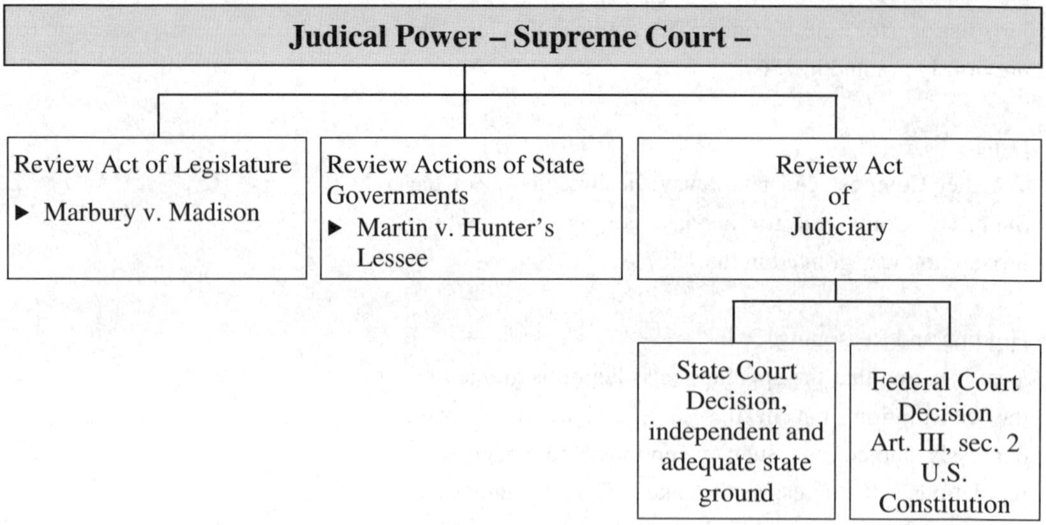

C. Limitations on Exercise of Federal Jurisdiction

Even if a federal court has jurisdiction over the subject matter of a case, it still might refuse to hear the case. Whether the court will hear the case depends on whether limitations on jurisdiction are present. There are mainly three issues to discuss:

sachliche Zuständigkeit

Beschränkungen der Zuständigkeit

- **standing**
- **mootness**
- **ripeness**

I. Standing

Probably the most important rule about when the federal courts may hear a case is that they may do so only when the plaintiff has "standing" to assert his claim. That means that the **plaintiff must have a significant stake in the controversy**.

verhandeln

einen Anspruch geltend machen

Anteil

1. Requirement of "Injury in Fact"

The key concept behind the law of standing is simple: the litigant must show that he has suffered an **"injury in fact"**. At its broadest level, the standing requirement means that the plaintiff must show that he has himself been injured in some way by the conduct that he complains of.

Prozesspartei – erleiden
Verhalten – beklagen

2. Plaintiffs Without Standing

The standing rules tend to keep two main types of cases out of the federal courts:

Bundesgerichte

- **non-individuated harm**: First, there are cases in which the harm suffered by the plaintiff is no different from that suffered by very large numbers of people not before the court.
- **third parties' rights**: Second, there are cases where the rights claimed to be violated are not the rights of the plaintiff, but instead the rights of third parties who are not before the court.

verletzt

3. Taxpayer and Citizen Suits

The most important context in which standing problems arise are suits that are brought by federal "citizens" or **"taxpayers" arguing that their general rights as citizens or taxpayers are violated by governmental action**.

Prozess
Steuerzahler
Regierungs-

a) Taxpayer Suits

Suppose that the plaintiff contends that he is a federal taxpayer, and that his tax dollars are being spent by the government in some illegal way. May the plaintiff pursue this suit in federal court? In general, the answer will be, "no". The fact that a person's federal taxes are used to fund an unconstitutional or illegal government program is simply **not a sufficient connection** with the governmental action to confer **standing** on the plaintiff.

behaupten
illegal – Kläger – verfolgen
finanzieren
Verbindung
übertragen

Frothingham v. Mellon – 262 U.S. 447 (1923)	
A federal taxpayer disagreed with the Treasury expenditures in a Congressional Act. He felt that it exceeded the general power of the Congress and thereby invaded the province of the states under the 10th amendment.	Finanzministerium Ausgabe allgemeine Zuständigkeit verletzen – Bereich
The taxpayer filed suit challenging the act under the theory that as a taxpayer, he would have property taken without due process, because the expenditure would result in an increase, generally, in his taxes.	angreifen, herausfordern ordnungsgemäßes Verfahren
Issue	
Whether a single federal taxpayer has standing to sue the federal government to prevent expenditures if his only injury is an anticipated increase in taxes?	klagen abhalten erwartet
Holding and Reasoning	
No. The taxpayer's interest in the treasury money is shared with millions of others and is too small to determine. There are too many uncertain and fluctuating factors to determine the effect this act might have on one person's taxes. Furthermore, if we decide this case, where there is no controversy, we would assume a position of review of the governmental acts of another co-equal department. That would be an authority which the court does not possess.	Mittel des Finanzministers bestimmen schwanken annehmen Macht, Zuständigkeit

b) Citizen Suits

If the plaintiff argues that he is a federal "citizen", and that as such he has the right to have his government act in accordance with the Constitution, and if the plaintiff has no direct connection with the governmental act he is complaining about, the plaintiff will not have standing. The Court has always held that one federal citizen's interest in lawful government is no different from the interest of any other citizen, and that an individual litigant relying on citizenship has not shown the "individualized" injury-in-fact that is required for standing.	beklagen entscheiden Prozesspartei sich verlassen

4. Cases not Based on Taxpayer or Citizen Status

Besides these taxpayer and citizen cases there are many ordinary law suits, where standing plays a role.
There are three standing requirements that the plaintiff must meet:

- he must show that he has suffered (or is likely to suffer) an **"injury in fact"**; — wahrscheinlich
- the injury he is suffering must be concrete and **"individuated"**; and — individualisierbar
- the action being challenged must be the **"cause in fact"** of the injury. — angegriffen

a) "Injury in Fact"

The plaintiff must show that he either has suffered, or will probably suffer, some concrete "injury in fact". This "injury in fact" requirement is pretty **loosely applied**. For instance, the harm does not have to be economic in nature. If the plaintiff has not already suffered the injury in fact, he must show that the future injury is not only probable but "concrete" and "imminent". In other words, a **vague sort of harm** that may come about in the indefinite future **will not suffice**.

Anforderung – weit auslegen
wahrscheinlich
bevorstehend

Lujan v. Defenders of Wildlife – 504 U.S. 555 (1992)

The Endangered Species Act of 1973 (§7(a)(2)) required deferral agencies to consult with the Secretary of the Interior to ensure that any authorized actions did not jeopardize endangered or threatened species or critically destroy natural habitats. A 1986 amendment to the act limited its scope to actions in the United States or on the high seas. Defenders of Wildlife and other organizations dedicated to wildlife conservation filed an action seeking a declaratory judgment that the new amendment erred by providing for a geographic limit on the original law.

Innenminister
gefährden – gefährdet
Lebensraum
widmen
Feststellungsurteil – irren

Issue
Do the respondents have standing to sue?

Holding and Reasoning
No. Even if the Court were to assume that the agency-funded projects at issue threatened listed species, there was no proof that these actions would produce "actual or imminent" injuries to particular respondents who might some day wish to visit the foreign countries in question. The Court disregarded the proposed theory of "ecosystem nexus" which claimed that any person who used any part of a "contiguous ecosystem" adversely affected by a funded activity had standing to sue.

Beklagter

ablehnen

benachbart – nachteilig

b) Individuated Harm

The harm that has been or will be suffered by the plaintiff has to be "individuated". That is, it cannot be the same harm as suffered by every citizen, or every taxpayer.

c) Causation

Finally, the action that the plaintiff is complaining about must be the "cause in fact" of his injury. Actually, this causation requirement breaks down into two sub-requirements: the plaintiff has to show that the challenged action was a **"but for" cause of his injury**, that is, that the injury would not have occurred unless the challenged action had taken place; and the plaintiff must show that a favorable decision in the suit will probably **redress the injury to him**.

Erfordernis – unterteilen

conditio sine qua non
eintreten

günstige – beseitigen, abhelfen

II. Mootness

Another limit on Supreme Court's review: the concept of mootness.

1. General Rule

A case may not be heard by the federal courts if it is "moot". A case is moot if it raised a live controversy at the time the complaint was filed, but **events occurring after the filing** have deprived the litigant of an ongoing stake in the controversy.

einreichen
vorenthalten – Anteil

DeFunis v. Odegaard – 416 U.S. 312 (1974)

DeFunis was denied admission to the University of Washington Law School despite test scores that were higher than some of the minorities admitted. DeFunis then successfully asked a trial court to require the school to admit him. On appeal, the Washington Supreme Court reversed, upholding the school's decision to deny DeFunis admission. The U.S. Supreme Court considered the case as DeFunis was entering his final year of school.

Minderheiten – zulassen
erfordern
Berufung
beurteilen

Issue
Was the case in question moot and therefore outside the scope of judicial review?

Holding and Reasoning
In a 5-4 per curiam opinion, the Court held that because the University of Washington Law School had agreed to allow DeFunis to enroll and to earn a diploma, the case in question was moot. DeFunis would be able to complete his legal studies irrespective of any Supreme Court decision. The controversy between parties had thus "clearly ceased to be 'definite and concrete' and no longer 'touch[ed] the legal relations of parties having adverse legal interests".'

einschreiben – ein Diplom bekommen
unabhängig
aufhören
Parteien
entgegengesetzt

Apparently the rule that the federal courts may not decide "moot" cases is required by the Constitution. That is, deciding a case when the parties no longer have a live controversy would amount to issuing an advisory opinion, in violation of Article III's "case or controversy" requirement.

erlassen – empfehlend

2. Exceptions

The courts recognize a few situations where a case that would appear to be "moot" will nonetheless be heard.

a) Pregnancy

For instance, a case will not be treated as moot if the issue it raises is **"capable of <u>repetition</u>, yet <u>evading</u> review"**. This "capable of repetition, yet evading review" doctrine takes care of situations in which, if the case were to be declared moot, a different person might be injured in the same way by the same defendant, and his claim, too, would be mooted before review could be had.

Wiederholung – entgehen

This was held in **Roe v. Wade** (infra, page 77), where the pregnant plaintiff wanted to terminate her pregnancy by abortion in 1970. The case was heard by the Supreme Court in 1973. A <u>pregnancy</u> will almost always be over before the usual <u>appellate process</u> is complete. Therefore, if the Court <u>insisted</u> that the named plaintiff who starts the suit must still be pregnant by the time the suit gets to the Supreme Court, no plaintiff could ever get to that Court. So the constitutionality of the Texas anti-abortion law is "capable of repetition, yet evading review".

Schwangerschaft
Berufungsverfahren
auf etwas bestehen

b) Voluntary Cessation by Defendant

The case will generally not be treated as moot if the defendant voluntarily ceases the <u>conduct</u> that the plaintiff is complaining about. So if the plaintiff is seeking an <u>injunction</u>, the defendant cannot usually get the case <u>dismissed</u> on mootness grounds merely by saying that he has voluntarily stopped the conduct that the plaintiff is trying to get an injunction against — unless the defendant shows that there is no **<u>reasonable likelihood</u>** that he will return to his old ways, the court will let the <u>action</u> go forward.

Verhalten

einstweilige Verfügung
abweisen

angemessene Wahrschein-lichkeit – Klage

<u>III. Ripeness</u>

The concept of <u>ripeness</u> is the opposite of mootness. A case is moot, because it no longer involves an actual controversy. By contrast, a case is not yet ripe (and therefore not yet decidable by a federal court) if it has not yet become sufficiently concrete to be easily <u>adjudicated</u>.

Entscheidungsreife

entscheiden

One common ripeness problem arises where the plaintiff attacks the constitutionality of a statute and says that he has violated the statute, but it is clear that **the statute is rarely enforced and probably will not be enforced in this particular situation**. If the court believes that it is very unlikely that the statute will be enforced against the plaintiff either for the activity he has already done or similar activity he is likely to do in the future, the court will probably treat the case as being not ripe.

Verfassungsmäßigkeit – Gesetz

Geltung verschaffen

Diagram 10

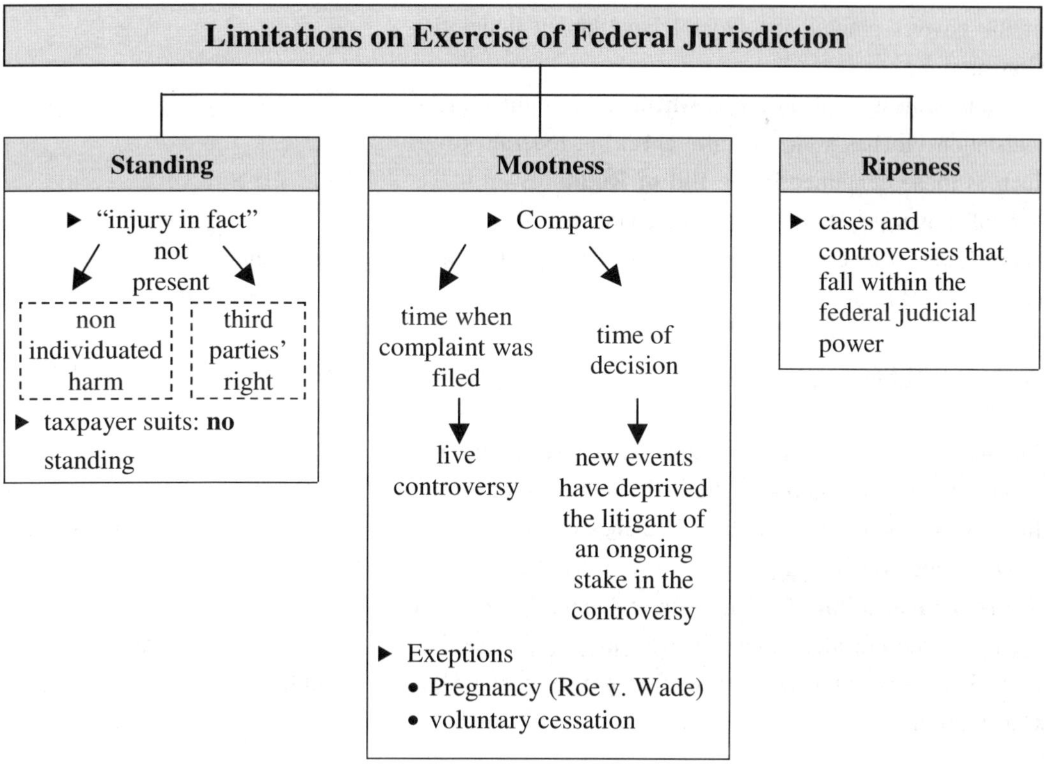

Part 3: Federalism and Federal Power

Federalism has been discussed in the introductory chapter. The United States has a "federalist" system. In other words, the national government and the state governments co-exist. Whereas the federal (or national) government has only those powers granted to it by the Constitution, **the state governments are governments of "unlimited" powers**, having all powers not prohibited to them by the Constitution.

koexistieren

In order to determine whether any action of the federal government complies with the Constitution, the federal action must be reviewed on two bases. First, it must be determined whether the enactment is made pursuant to one of the powers granted the federal government under the Constitution.

Second, it must be determined whether the regulation or legislation violates some specific check on federal power such as those contained in the **Bill of Rights**. Even if the federal government is acting pursuant to one of its enumerated powers, it may not disregard these constitutional limitations.

missachten

A. System of Enumerated Powers

aufgezählt

The most important principle in this whole area is that the federal government is one of limited, enumerated powers. In other words, the three federal branches can only assert **powers specifically granted to them by the United States Constitution**. So any time Congress passes a statute, or the President issues an Executive Order one has to look for the enumerated, specified power in the U.S. Constitution.

Staatsgewalten auf Bundesebene
zuteilen

Gesetz – Verwaltungsentscheidung

I. No General Police Power

The most dramatic illustration of this state/federal difference is the general "police power". Each state has a general police power, i.e., the ability to regulate solely on

Darstellung, Abbildung

the basis that the regulation would enhance the welfare of the citizenry. But there is no general federal police power, i.e., no right of the federal government to regulate for the health, safety or general welfare of the citizenry. Instead, each act of federal legislation or regulation must come within one of the very specific, enumerated powers (e.g., the Commerce Clause, the power to tax and spend, etc.).

Bürgerschaft
regulieren

II. "Necessary and Proper" Clause

In addition to the very specific powers given to Congress by the Constitution, the Constitution also includes an "open provision" in art. I, § 8:

> *"Congress shall have the power [...] to make all laws which shall be* ***necessary and proper*** *for carrying into execution the foregoing powers, and all other powers vested by this Constitution in the Government of the United States, or in any Department or Officer thereof".*

angemessen
zustehen

The "Necessary and Proper" Clause means that if Congress is seeking an objective that is within the specifically enumerated powers, then Congress can use any means that is rationally related to the objective Congress is trying to achieve, and is not specifically forbidden by the Constitution.

sich beziehen auf

III. No Violation of Constitutional Provisions

Even where Congressional action appears to fall within a specific grant of power, the federal action may not, of course, violate some other specific constitutional guarantee. In other words, Congressional (or other federal) action must satisfy two tests to be constitutional:

- it must fall within some specific grant of power under the Constitution; and
- it must not violate any specific constitutional provision

scheinen
verletzen – Verfassungs-
Gewährung

Diagram 11

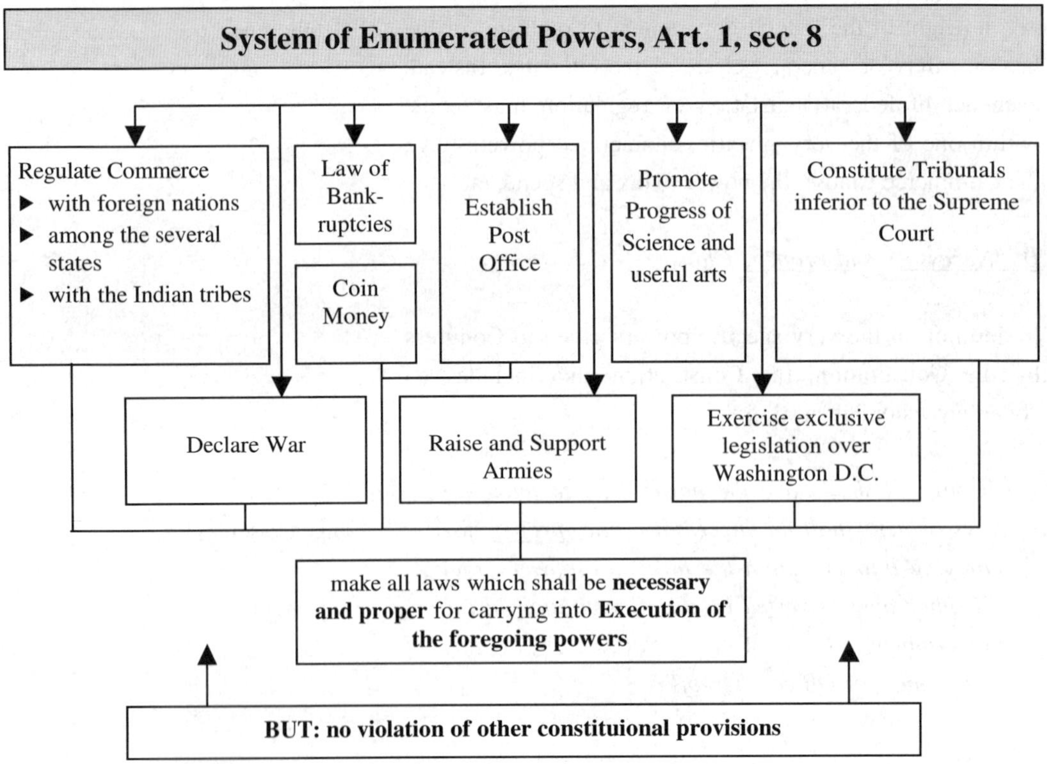

B. Constitutional Interpretation

Whatever labels might be given to the Court's approaches to constitutional interpretation? Acharacteristic of most of them is that they are very flexible. This is at odds with the common law approach to the interpretation of statutes under which courts in the United States generally view **statutes as stating particular legal rules and nothing more**. Much of the body of constitutional caselaw cannot be traced to the text of the Constitution by any traditional means of interpretation that are applied to other forms of enacted law.

mit etwas in Konflikt stehen

aufgespürt, verfolgt

The tendency toward a flexible and expansive approach to constitutional interpretation is most often associated with the constitutional "rights explosion" of the 1960s, but in

Tendenz – Ansatz

many ways it has existed virtually from the beginning. In 1819, in *McCulloch v. Maryland*, Chief Justice Marshall found **"implied powers" behind those specifically enumerated to sustain the constitutionality of a federal statute**. Further, he reasoned from the overall structure of the Constitution to find an immunity of the federal government from oppressive state taxation.

aufrechterhalten

Immunität

McCulloch v. Maryland, 17 U.S. 316 (1819)

In 1816, Congress chartered the Second Bank of the United States, which became active in Maryland. In 1818, the Maryland legislature passed an Act to tax any bank not chartered by the Legislature of Maryland, thus taxing the U.S. Bank. The law provided for private remedies against the bank operators, of which, one was McCulloch. The trial court entered judgment on the basis of an agreed statement of facts (that the U.S. Bank was not chartered by the Maryland legislature), and the Maryland Court of Appeal affirmed. An appeal was taken by writ of error to the Supreme Court.

gründen

Anspruch, Ersatz

urteilen

Issues

1) Whether Congress has the power to incorporate a bank; and 2) Whether the state of Maryland may, without violating the constitution, tax the U.S. Bank?

gründen

Holding and Reasoning

Marshall first noted that the Congressional power established by the Constitution originates from the people, not the states. Article II should be read in light of the previous Articles of Confederation, which were unworkable because of their strict limitations on express Congressional power. The Constitution, by nature, must be general in order to adapt to unforeseen circumstances. Thus, there must be some implied powers to allow Congress to exercise the broad range of express powers given as means to ends. The language "necessary and proper" should be construed to mean "convenient, or

Konföderationsartikel

Grenzen

angleichen, anpassen

useful, or essential" not as things that are absolutely necessary, otherwise the word "proper" would be superfluous, and there would be no need to include the word "absolutely" in the enumeration of powers to the states. The "necessary and proper" language is included among the power of Congress, not the limitations, and so should be read as enlarging the scope of Congress' powers. All means which are appropriate and plainly adapted to the exercise of enumerated powers are constitutional, not just those that are strictly necessary. As to whether Maryland could tax the federal bank, the power to tax something is the power to destroy it. Since the states are necessarily inferior to the federal government, the states do not have the power to "destroy" (by taxing) the federal government. The people did not design to make their federal government dependent on the states.

überflüssig
vergrößern
Möglichkeiten
untergeordnet
abhängig

Thus, the Supreme Court interpreted the **Necessary and Proper Clause** so as to establish the legitimate role of federal government in dealing with national problems.

errichten, einrichten

C. Federal Commerce Power

I. Introduction

Probably Congress' most important power is the power to

> *"regulate Commerce with foreign nations, and among the several states, and with the Indian Tribes"*. (Art. I, § 8)

This is the **"Commerce Clause"**. The brevity of this clause verifies the fact that its interpretation has played a significant role in shaping the concepts of federalism and the permissible uses of national power throughout American history.

Kürze

The federal government was granted neither a general police power nor the inherent right to act on any subject matter in order to promote the health, safety or welfare of the people throughout the nation. But as the framers did grant Congress a power to regulate commerce the commerce clause adjudication is the history of the concepts of federalism as well as the development of doctrines supporting a specific federal power.

gewähren
innewohnend
Verfassungsväter
Rechtsprechung

II. Elements

There seem to be three broad categories of activities which Congress can constitutionally regulate under the Commerce power:

weit, breit

1. Channels

First, Congress can regulate the **use of the "channels" of interstate commerce**. Thus Congress can regulate in a way that is reasonably related to highways, waterways, and air traffic. Presumably Congress can do so even though the activity in question in the particular case is completely intrastate.

Kanal
innerstaatlich

2. Instrumentalities

Second, Congress can regulate the **"instrumentalities" of interstate commerce**, even though the particular activities being regulated are completely intrastate. This category refers to people, machines, and other "things" used in carrying out commerce.

3. "Substantially Affecting" Commerce

Finally, the biggest (and most interesting) category is that Congress may regulate those activities having a **"substantial effect" on interstate commerce**.

United States v. Lopez, 514 U.S. 549 (1995)

Lopez was a high school senior in San Antonio who was caught with a .38 caliber handgun and five bullets on school grounds. Lopez was charged with violation of § 922(q) of the Gun-Free School Zones Act of 1990, which made it a federal offense "for any individual knowingly to possess a firearm at a...school zone". The District Court convicted him on a bench trial and sentenced him to six months' imprisonment. The Court of Appeal for the 5th district reversed the conviction on the grounds that the law was unconstitutional as being beyond the power of Congress to legislate control over local public schools, and the Supreme Court granted certiorari.

Kugeln, Patronen
beschuldigen
Vergehen
verurteilen
Gefängnis

Issue

Whether § 922(q) of the Gun-Free School Zones Act is unconstitutional as being beyond the power of Congress to legislate control over local public schools?

Holding and Reasoning

§ 922(q) is a criminal statute that has no observable relationship to "commerce" or any sort of economic enterprise, regardless of how broadly those terms are defined. Deterring the presence of guns on school grounds is not part of a larger regulatory scheme to control commerce that would otherwise be undermined if not viewed in the "aggregate". Furthermore, it contains no test by which the firearm in question could be rationally linked to interstate commerce. Although the lack of formal Congressional findings to this extent are not fatal, their absence fails to save the statute from the otherwise plain observation that it is not commerce-related. To accept the government's position that guns at schools do have a substantial effect on commerce because they adversely affect the economy would be to give virtually unlimited power to Congress to regulate any activity that has a social cost. Additionally, such a

bemerkenswert, erkennbar
Unternehmen
abschrecken
verhängnisvoll – Fehlen

position would allow Congress to provide federally mandated school curriculums, and regulate each and every aspect of local schools. This is too broad a reading of the commerce power. — weit, breit

Dissent Reasoning: [Souter]

> David H. Souter (1939 –)
> Ass. Justice: 1990 –
> Party: Republican
> Appointed by: G. W. Bush, sen.

The Court was wrong to second-guess the rational basis for Congress' enactment of this Act based on the commerce clause. As a matter of judicial restraint, the Court should defer judgment to the legislature when it appears that there is a rational basis for the Act. — Be-, Einschränkung – verschieben, verweisen

If the activity itself is arguably "commercial", then it does not seem to matter whether the particular instance of the activity directly affects interstate commerce, as long as the instance is part of a general class of activities that, collectively, substantially affect interstate commerce. So even **purely intrastate activities can be regulated if they are directly "commercial"**. — Fall; innerstaatlich

The Supreme Court has sustained congressional power to regulate any activity, local or interstate, that either in itself or in combination with other activities has a substantial economic effect upon, or effect on movement in interstate commerce.

Wickard v. Filburn, 317 U.S. 111 (1942)

Filburn was a small farmer in Ohio. He was given a wheat acreage allotment of 11.1 acres under a Department of Agriculture directive which authorized the government to set production quotas for wheat. Filburn harvested nearly 12 acres of wheat above his allotment. He claimed that he wanted the wheat for use on his farm, including feed for his poultry and livestock. Fiburn was penalized. He argued that the excess wheat was unrelated to commerce since he grew it for his own use. — Weizen – Parzelle, Zuteilung; ernten; Geflügel – Vieh; bestraft

Issue

Is the amendment subjecting Filburn to acreage restrictions in violation of the Constitution because Congress has no power to regulate activities local in nature?

Holding and Reasoning

Robert H. Jackson (1892-1954) Ass. Justice: 1941-1954 Party: Democrat Nominated: F. D. Roosevelt

According to Filburn, the act regulated production and consumption, which are local in character. The rule laid down by Justice Jackson is that even if an activity is local and not regarded as commerce, "it may still, whatever its nature, be reached by Congress if it exerts a substantial economic effect on interstate commerce, and this irrespective of whether such effect is what might at some earlier time have been defined as 'direct' or 'indirect".'

unbeachtlich

III. State and Local Government Immunity

Now, the question is whether the Court should use federalism principles to create doctrines that would provide states with immunity from federal commercial regulatory laws. The court's current position denies state and local governments constitutional immunity from most, if not all, federal legislation.
The **Tenth Amendment** provides that

> *"the powers not delegated to the United States by the Constitution, nor prohibited by it to the States, are reserved to the States respectively, or to the People".*

This Amendment today seems to place a small but possibly significant limit on Congress' ability to use its commerce power to regulate the states.
In 1985, in *Garcia v. San Antonio Metropolitan Transit Authority*, the Court overruled prior case law and held that **neither the Tenth Amendment nor the structure of the federal system justified restriction of Congress' power to apply otherwise valid commercial regulations to state or local governments**.

gültig

Garcia v. San Antonio Metropolitan Transit Authority (SAMTA) – 469 U.S. 528 (1985)

Garcia was a bus driver who worked overtime hours. Under the FLSA (Fair Labor Standards Act), SAMTA was required to pay a certain wage and comply with certain overtime standards. However, four months after the Supreme Court's ruling in *National League of Cities v. Usery (426 U.S. 833)*, that the FLSA did not apply to state government agencies "in areas of traditional government functions", SAMTA notified its employees that the decision relieved it of its overtime obligations under the FLSA because a municipal public mass-transit system was traditionally a local government function, and therefore immune from FLSA. — erleichtern

Garcia sued for his overtime pay under the FLSA. The District Court found that a municipal operation of a mass transit system was a traditional government function, and thus under *National League of Cities*, is exempt from the FLSA wage and overtime obligations. — klagen

Issue

Whether Congress has the power, under the Commerce Clause, to regulate activities and functions that are "traditionally" an "integral" part of state government operations? — zentral, vollständig

Holding and Reasoning

Yes. The fundamental limitation that the constitutional scheme imposes on Congress' power under the commerce clause to protect "states as states" from intrusion by federal regulation is a procedural one to be found in the political process - states' and citizens' participation in federal governmental action. — Störung

The test of National League of Cities, that Congress may not interfere with "traditional" state government functions, is unworkable. There is no meaningful way to determine what is a "traditional" or "integral" part of a state government's function, and what is not. Such an approach has led to artificial results since its enactment. History is not a viable ground for a determination because this prevents meaningful change when necessary, as well as being fairly arbitrary. Furthermore, it requires the unelected judiciary to review legislative decisions based on which policies it likes and dislikes. — sinnvoll; willkürlich

If Congress has a particular power, it does not matter whether it interferes with the laws of the states. To find limits on the commerce power, the constitution itself must be examined. Since there are no express limits, the constitution suggests that the structure of the federal government itself is the process by which it is regulated; i.e. by state representatives to the federal government. The states' interests are best protected by their own representation in the federal government. Since the FLSA is a lesser burden on the states than many other Acts, it is evidence of the political pressures on the federal government to protect states' rights. Thus, *National League of Cities* is overruled.

interferes: stören, beeinträchtigen

evidence: Beweis

Dissent Reasoning

[O'Connor] felt that the majority had backed down from the fight for states' rights just when the states needed help from the Supreme Court. There is now a risk that Congress will gradually erase the diffusion of power between state and nation on which the Framers relied. Such a fear is not unwarranted given the amount of similar legislative activity in the last 30 years. The proper test should be weighing the states' rights as a "relevant consideration" in determining the constitutionality of uses of the commerce power.

Sandra Day O'Connor (1930 –) Ass. Justice: 1981 – Party: Republican Nominated by: Reagan

erase – diffusion: löschen – Verbreitung

Framers – unwarranted: Verfassungsväter – ungerechtfertigt

Diagram 12

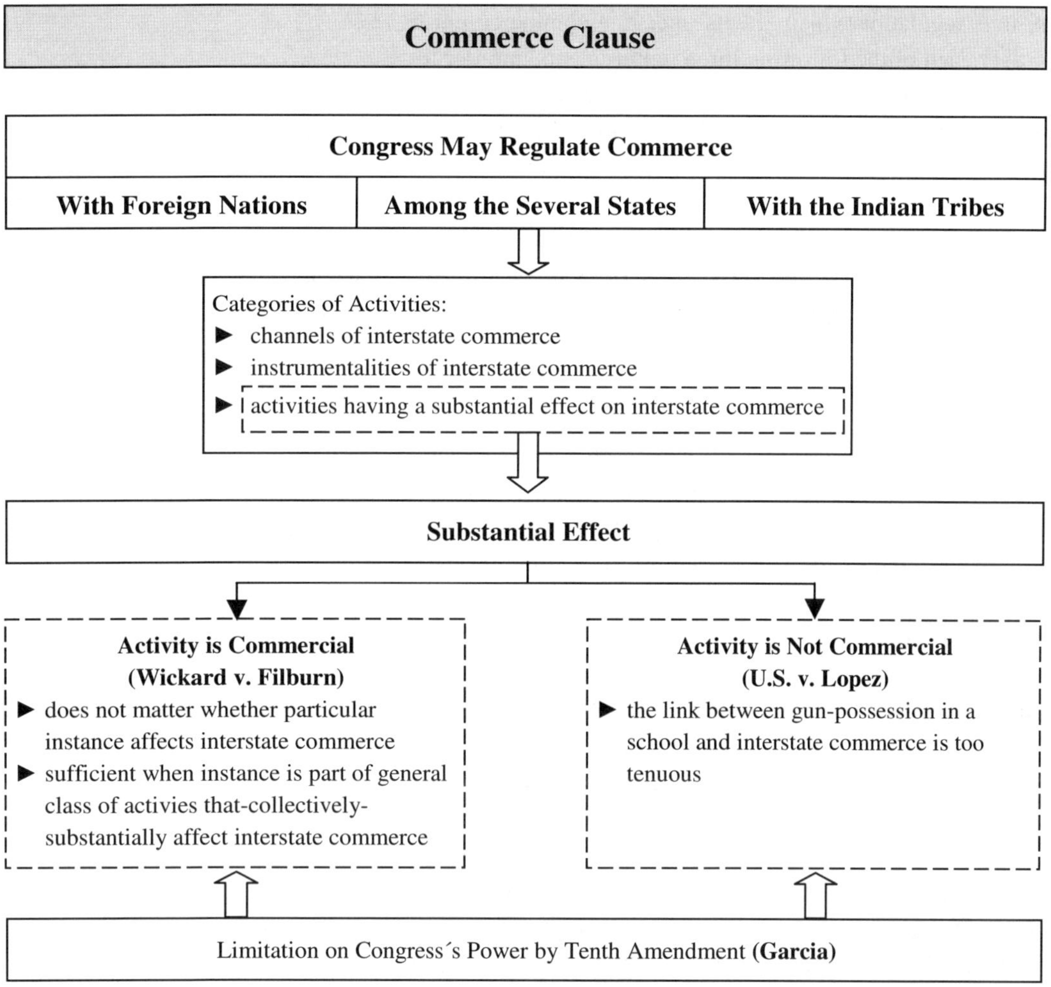

IV. Dormant Commerce Clause

The mere existence of the federal commerce power restricts the states from discriminating against, or unduly burdening, interstate commerce. This restriction is called the "**Dormant Commerce Clause**". innerstaatl. Handel

1. Three Part Test

A state regulation which affects interstate commerce must satisfy each of the following three requirements in order to avoid violating the Dormant Commerce Clause:

- The regulation must pursue a **legitimate state end**; — verfolgen – Ziel
- The regulation must be **rationally related** to that legitimate state end; and
- The regulatory burden imposed by the state on interstate commerce must be **outweighed by the state's interest** in enforcing its regulation. — gewichtiger sein; durchsetzen

2. Discrimination Against Out-of-Staters

Above all else, the dormant commerce clause comes into play for **intentional discrimination against out-of-staters**. If the state is promoting its residents' own economic interests, this will not be a legitimate state objective, so the regulation will virtually automatically violate the Commerce Clause. — fördern; Zielsetzung

Hood & Sons, Inc. v. DuMond – 336 U.S. 525 (1939)

The Hood Company, a Massachusetts company, owned three milk-receiving stations in New York. The company distributed milk from these facilities in Boston. When the company sought a license for another receiving station in New York, state officials denied its request on the grounds that expanding Hood's facilities would reduce the local supply of milk and result in destructive competition. The company appealed the case to the Supreme Court. — suchen; zerstörerisch Wettbewerb

Issue

Was New York's denial of the license unconstitutional under the Commerce Clause?

Holding and Reasoning

Yes. In a 5-to-4 decision, the Court held that New York's restriction on business activity was an unconstitutional application of the Commerce Clause. The Court held that the system fostered by the Clause must be one in which "every farmer and every craftsman shall be encouraged to produce by the certainty he will have free access to every market in the Nation". The Court also emphasized the economic interdependence of the states, warning that "fantastic rivalries...and reprisals" would ensue if the states were allowed to enact local protectionist measures.

pflegen
Handwerker
Vergeltung – nachfolgen

3. Health/Safety/Welfare Regulations

Regulations that are truly addressed to the state's health, safety and welfare objectives are usually "legitimate".

4. Balancing Test

When one performs the balancing part of the test (to see whether the benefits to the state from its regulation outweigh the unintentional burdens to commerce), one always has to look whether there are less restrictive means available to the state: if the state could accomplish its objective as well (or even almost as well) while burdening commerce less, then it probably has to do so.

unbeabsichtigt
Möglichkeiten
erreichen

5. Some Contexts

The most standard illustrations of forbidden protectionism are where the state says, "You can't bring your goods into our state", or "You can't take goods out of our state into your state". Here are some other contexts where Dormant Commerce Clause analysis may be important:

a) Embargo of Natural Resources

Laws that prevent scarce natural resources from moving out of the state where they are found are closely scrutinized. Often, this is **just protectionism** (e.g., a state charges higher taxes on oil destined for out-of-state than for in-state use.) But even if the state's interest is conservation or ecology, the measure will probably be struck down if **less-discriminatory alternatives** are available.

knapp
genau prüfen

b) Environmental Regulations

Similarly, the states may not protect their environment at the expense of their neighbors, unless there is no less-discriminatory way to achieve the same result.

City of Philadelphia v. New Jersey – 437 U.S. 617 (1978)

A New Jersey law prohibited the importation of most "solid or liquid waste which originated or was collected outside the territorial limits of the State". — Abfall

Issue

Did New Jersey's waste importation law violate the Commerce Clause?

Holding and Reasoning

Yes. The Court held that the law violated the principle of nondiscrimination as it treated out-of-state waste differently than waste produced within the state. Since New Jersey could not demonstrate a legitimate reason for distinguishing between foreign and domestically produced waste, it was clear to the Court that the state had "overtly moved to slow or freeze the flow of commerce for protectionist reasons".

legitimate — rechtmäßig, berechtigt
domestically — innerstaatlich

V. State Taxation of Interstate Commerce

Just as state regulation may be found to unduly burden (or discriminate against) interstate commerce, so state taxation may be found to unduly burden or discriminate against interstate commerce, and thus violate the Commerce Clause. To strike a state tax as violative of the Commerce Clause, the challenger must generally show either discrimination or that it is burdensome.

violative — verletzend
challenger — Angreifer
burdensome — belastend

1. Discrimination

The challenger must show that the state is discriminating against interstate commerce, by taxing in a way that **unjustifiably benefits local commerce** at the expense of out-of-state commerce.

expense — Aufwand, Ausgabe

2. Burdensome

Furthermore, it must be shown that the state's taxing scheme (perhaps taken in conjunction with other states' taxing schemes) unfairly burdens interstate commerce even though it **does not discriminate on its face**. One way this can happen is if the tax leads to unfair <u>cumulative</u> taxation. kumulativ The test is whether, if every state applied the same tax, commerce would be unduly burdened.

Diagram 13

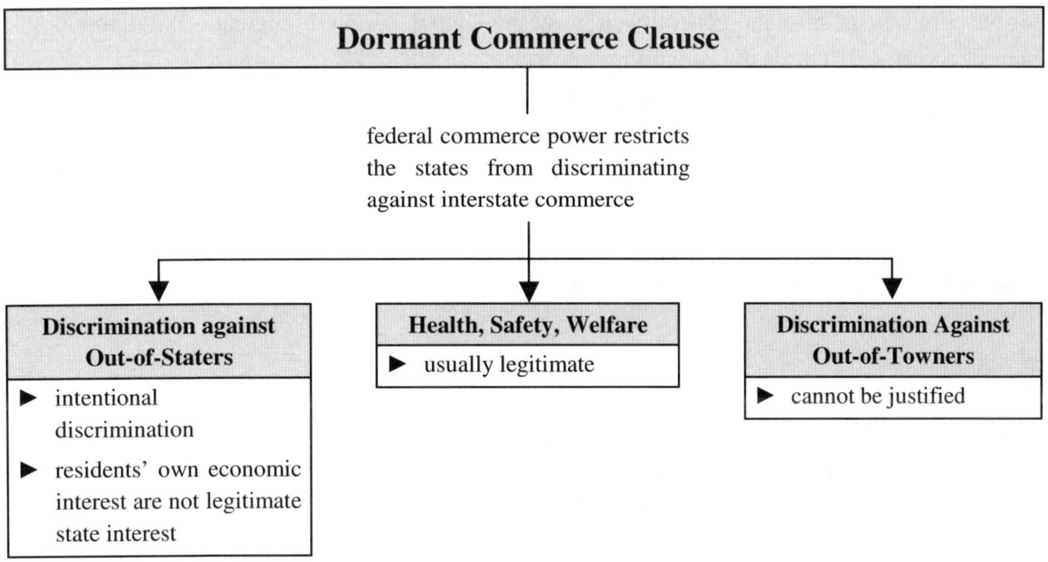

<u>D. Other National Powers</u>

The Constitution establishes other sources of federal power which, although litigated less frequently, have resulted in Supreme Court decisions clarifying the extent of federal power.

<u>*I. Taxing Power*</u>

Congress has the power to **"lay and collect taxes"** (Art. 1, § 8). This is an independent source of congressional power, so it can be used to reach conduct that might be beyond the other sources of congressional power, like the Commerce Clause.

The requirement of uniformity in the levy of indirect taxes has been interpreted by the Court to mean geographical uniformity only. — Erhebung; auslegen

"Direct taxes" must be allocated among the states in proportion to population. A "direct" tax has seldom been employed by Congress. — zuordnen; anwenden

II. Spending Power

Congress also has the power to "pay the debts and provide for the common defense and general welfare of the United States". (Art I, § 8) This is the **"spending" power**. — Schulden; Verteidigung – Wahlfahrt

This is an independent power, just like the Commerce power. So Congress could spend to achieve a purely local benefit, even one that it couldn't achieve by regulating under the Commerce power.

United States v. Butler – 297 U.S. 1 (1936)

As part of the 1933 Agricultural Adjustment Act, Congress implemented a processing tax on agricultural commodities, from which funds would be redistributed to farmers who promised to reduce their acreage. The Act intended to solve the crisis in agricultural commodity prices which was causing many farmers to go under. — Verarbeitung; Erzeugnis

Issue

Did Congress exceed its constitutional taxing and spending powers with the Act? — überschreiten

Holding and Reasoning

Yes. The Court found the Act unconstitutional because it attempted to regulate and control agricultural production, an arena reserved to the states. Even though Congress does have the power to tax and appropriate funds, argued Justice Roberts, in this case those activities were "but means to an unconstitutional end", and violated the Tenth Amendment.

III. The War, Treaty and Foreign Affairs Power

Article 1, Section 8 gives Congress the power to declare war, raise and support armies, provide for and maintain a navy, and make rules for the government and regulation of the armed forces.

erklären, ausrufen
Marine unterhalten

From the time that the Constitution was adopted until modern times, Congress has only passed six declarations of war:

- The **War of 1812**, declaration passed on June 18, 1812
- **Barbary Wars**, declaration passed on March 3, 1815
- **Mexican War**, declaration passed on May 13, 1846
- **Spanish-American War**, declaration passed on April 25, 1846
- **World War I**, declarations passed on April 6 (Germany) and December 11 (Austria-Hungary), 1917
- **World War II**, declarations passed on December 8 (Japan) and December 11 (Germany and Italy), 1941

There was no declaration of war for the Korean War in the early 1950s, Vietnam in the 1960s or the war with Iraq in February and March of 1991.

Regulatory power of Congress, especially in economic matters and mobilization of troops, in support of war effort is pervasive; thus, the Court has sustained national price and rent control, as well as conscription and regulation of civilian production and services. To a considerable extent, this pervasive regulatory power may be validly extended into post-wartime periods both to remedy and wartime disruptions.

regelnd
weitverbreitet – aufrechterhalten
Einziehung
Unterbrechung

Constitutional provisions confer the **treaty making power** to the federal government, specifically to the President and the Senate. Although there are no express limitations on treaty making in the text of the Constitution the Supreme Court has endeavored to define the scope of the treaty power.

Part 4: The Executive Power

The entire **"executive power"** is vested in the President by Article II, Section 1, of the Constitution. Various executive functions may be and are delegated within the "executive branch" by the President or by Congress.

übertragen, verleihen

abordnen

A. Execution of Laws

The President's power over internal affairs as the chief executive is unclear. Clearly the president has some power to direct subordinate executive officers, and there is a long history of presidents issuing executive orders. Perhaps the best guide for determining the validity of presidential actions regarding internal affairs can be based on Justice Jackson's opinion in the Steel Seizure case.

innere Angelegenheiten

untergeordnet

Vollzugsanordnung

Youngstown Sheet & Tube Co. v. Sawyer – 343 U.S. 579 (1952)

In the latter part of the Korean war, labor disputes led to a threatened strike by the steel workers. President Truman issued an executive order directing the Secretary of Commerce to seize the steel mills and keep them running. The Secretary issued orders to the presidents of the steel companies, directing them to keep the mills open. The next morning, the President sent a message to Congress reporting his action and promising to abide by their decision either way. Congress took no action. However, there was evidence that Congress disapproved of allowing the President to exercise such power because a few years prior, they removed a clause from the Taft-Hartley Act that would have given the President power to seize an industry in case of national emergency.

Harry S. Truman (1884-1972)
33rd President of the United States (Democrat): 1945-1953

Handelsminister

beschlagnahmen – Hochofen

anweisen

versprechen

sich halten an

Beweis

missbilligen

Issue

Whether the president had the power under these circumstances to seize the steel mills of the country?

Holding and Reasoning

No. There is no express power in the Constitution supporting the president's actions. The government claims that the power should be implied from the aggregate of the presidential powers under the Constitution. However, the order cannot be sustained under the power of the Commander in Chief of the armed forces because that power is reserved for military commanders in the theater of war and is not broad enough to cover the situation here. This is a job for the nation's lawmakers, not the military authorities. Also, the president's power to see that the laws are faithfully executed refutes the idea that he is to be a lawmaker. Congress has the exclusive constitutional power to make laws necessary and proper to carry out the powers vested by the constitution in any officer thereof. Thus, this order is unconstitutional.

unterstützen
inbegriffen
Gesamtheit
vorbehalten
wortgetreu
widerlegen
ausführen – übertragen

Concurrence Reasoning

[Frankfurter] felt that the situation was more complicated and flexible. How ever, in view of the Taft-Hartley Act, Congress has expressed its will to withhold this power from the President in cases like this. In effect, the Congress has said, "ask for seizure power from us if you feel it is needed in a specific situation".

Felix Frankfurter (1882-1965)
Ass. Justice: 1939-1962
Party: Democrat
Appointed by: F.D. Roosevelt

Dissent Reasoning

The President has some power under the constitution to meet a critical situation in the absence of express statutory authorization. Looking at history (particularly WWII), there were several instances when the President made similar orders. The fact that Congress and the courts have consistently recognized and given their support to such executive action indicates that such a power of seizure has been accepted throughout our history.

anzeigen

B. Commander in Chief

Although lacking the power to declare or initiate a "formal" war, the President has **extensive military powers**. The President is Commander in Chief of the armed forces. So he directs and leads the armed forces. This power includes the establishment of military governments in occupied territories, including military tribunals.

fehlen
ausführlich, weitreichend
Ein-, Errichtung
Tribunal

C. Treaty and Foreign Affairs

The President can make treaties with foreign nations (but only if two-thirds of the Senate approves). All treaties "which shall be made under the authority of the United States are the supreme law of the land" (Article 6, Paragraph 2). Thus, it is clear that any state action or law in conflict with a United States treaty is invalid.

Executive orders and executive agreements are widely used in foreign affairs. Potential issues arise because the Constitution requires that treaties be ratified by the Senate, while executive agreements, which are not mentioned in the Constitution, do not. While many of the country's most important international commitments are still made by way of the formal treaty process, many commitments are made by way of executive agreement implemented by executive orders. The approach of the Court had been that these devices are permitted since the Constitution does not make treaties the exclusive form of international agreement. This is not necessarily a sign of a battle of wills between the President and Congress: the power to make executive agreements has often been authorized by ratified treaties or willingly delegated or otherwise approved by Congress. However, agreements that are not approved by Congress or made pursuant to a treaty sometimes test the outer limits of the President's power in foreign affairs.

The evidence of Congressional approval may be rather weak.

billigen
unwirksam
Abkommender Exekutive
erfordern – ratifizieren
Zugeständnis
einführen
Ansatz
Vorrichtung
"Krieg der Absichten"
gemäß – äußere Grenze

Dames & Moore v. Regan, 453 U.S. 654 (1981)

In reaction to the seizure of the U.S. embassy and American nationals in Iran, President Jimmy Carter invoked the International Emergency Economic Powers Act (IEEPA) and froze Iranian assets in the United States. When the hostages were released in 1981, President Ronald Reagan affirmed the agreements made by the Carter administration that terminated all legal proceedings against the Iranian government and created an independent Claims Tribunal. Dames & Moore attempted to recover over $3 million owed to it by the Iranian government and claimed the executive orders were beyond the scope of presidential power.

James E. Carter, Jr. (1924-)
39th President of the United States (Democrat): 1977-1981

Ronald Reagan (1911-2004)
40th President of the United States (Republican): 1981-1989

Beschlagnahme
einfrieren – Vermögen
Geisel
beenden
versuchen

Issue

Did the president have the authority to transfer Iranian funds and to nullify legal claims against Iran?

für null und nichtig erklären

Holding and Reasoning

Yes. The Court held that the International Emergency Economic Powers Act constituted a specific congressional authorization for the President to order the transfer of Iranian assets. The Court further held that although the IEEPA itself did not authorize the presidential suspension of legal claims, previous acts of Congress had "implicitly approved" of executive control of claim settlement. The Court emphasized the narrowness of its ruling, limiting the decision to the facts of the case.

darstellen
Vermögen
Sperre
Einigung – betonen

D. Appointment of Federal Officers

The President appoints all federal officers. These include **cabinet members** and **federal judges** (But the Senate must approve all such federal officers by majority vote.)

ernennen
Bundesrichter

As to "inferior [federal] officers", it's up to Congress to decide whether these should be appointed by the President, by the judicial branch, or by the "heads of departments" (i.e., cabinet members).

E. Pardons

The President can issue pardons, but only for federal offenses. Also, he cannot pardon anyone who has been impeached and convicted.

begnadigen
(Bundes-) Straftaten
unter Amtsanklage stellen

F. Veto

The President may veto any law passed by both houses (though this veto may be overridden by a two-third's majority of each house.) If the President does not veto the bill within 10 days after receiving it, it becomes law (unless Congress has adjourned by the 10th day after it sent him the bill — this is the so-called **"pocket veto"**).

untersagen – Kammer

Diagram 14

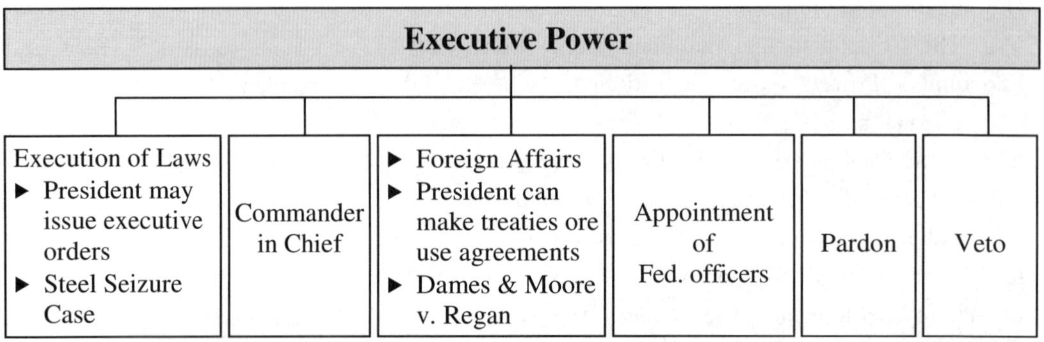

Part 5: Due Process of Law

A. Introduction

Both the **Fifth and the Fourteenth Amendment** prohibit governmental actions which would deprive "any person of life, liberty or property without due process of law".

The text of the 14th Amendment is the basis for due process. It provides that

Verfassungszusatz

> *"...no State shall make or enforce any law which shall abridge the privileges and immunities of citizens of the United States; nor shall any State deprive any person of life, liberty, or property, without due process of law; nor deny to any person within its jurisdiction the equal protection of the laws".*

But due process has several quite **distinct meanings**. On the one hand, due process restricts the ways in which the legislatures may limit individual freedom. This **"substantive"** due process may protect certain fundamental rights or void arbitrary limitations of individual freedom of action. Part of the substantive impact of the due process clause of the Fourteenth Amendment is the incorporation of certain guarantees in the Bill of Rights.

verschieden, klar

aufheben – willkürlich

Einfluss

The due process clauses also have a procedural aspect in that they guarantee that each person shall be accorded a **certain "process"** if they are deprived of life, liberty or property.

I. Due Process Clauses and Equal Protection

The Due Process Clauses and the Equal Protection Clause guarantee the fairness of laws – substantive due process guarantees the laws will be **reasonable and not arbitrary**, and equal protection guarantees that similarly situated persons will be **treated alike**. Both guarantees require the Court to review the substance of the law rather than the procedure employed.

willkürlich

gleich behandeln

Generally where a law limits the liberty of all persons to engage in some activity, it is a due process question. Where a law treats certain classes of people differently from others, it is an equal protection question.

sich betätigen

II. Applicable Tests

However, there are some basic principles for both clauses. The Court employs one of **three tests in reviewing laws under these clauses**, depending on the circumstances.	anwenden

1. Strict Scrutiny

The Court uses the strict scrutiny standard when a suspect classification or fundamental right is involved. Under the strict scrutiny standard, a law will be upheld only if it is necessary to achieve a **compelling and overriding government purpose**. The Court will always consider whether less burdensome means for accomplishing the legislative goal are available. Most governmental action examined under this test fails.	genaue Untersuchung – verdächtig schützen zwingend Möglichkeit – erreichen

2. Intermediate Scrutiny

The Court uses intermediate scrutiny when a classification based on gender or legitimacy is involved. Under the intermediate scrutiny standard, a law is upheld if it is substantially related to an **important government purpose**. In most cases the government has the burden of proof.	mittlere Untersuchung Geschlecht – Abstammung Beweislast

3. Rational Basis

The rational basis standard is used whenever the other two standards are not applicable. Under the rational basis standard, a law will be upheld if it is **rationally related to a legitimate interest**. It is difficult to fail this test; so most governmental action examined under this standard is upheld unless it is arbitrary or irrational.	rechtmäßig
In the first major section of this chapter it will be shown what interests the Supreme Court has held to come within the scope of the terms **"life", "liberty", or "property"**, for no process is required for government actions which do not deprive an individual of one of these three interests.	berauben, vorenthalten

In the second major section the types of procedures will be explained which are due an individual when the government takes an action which deprives him of one of these interests.

B. Substantive Due Process

The due process clauses apply only if a government action will constitute the impairment of some individual's life, liberty or property. Where government actions adversely affect an individual but do not constitute a denial of that individucal's life, liberty or property, the government does not have to give the person any hearing or process whatsoever. One might assume that the phrase "life, liberty or property" was to include all aspects of an individual's life in society, but the Supreme Court has given the phrase a more restrictive meaning.

Beeinträchtigung
einschränkend

I. Functions

The "substantive" component of the Due Process Clause derives mainly from the **interpretation of the term "liberty"** – certain types of state limits on human conduct have been held to so unreasonably interfere with important human rights that they amount to an unreasonable (and unconstitutional) denial of "liberty".

herleiten
Versagen

II. Rights Governed

1. Non-fundamental Rights

There is an absolutely critical distinction that one must make right at the outset, when one is analyzing a substantive due process problem. That's the distinction between **fundamental and non-fundamental rights**. If a right or value is found to be "non-fundamental", then the state action that impairs that right only has to meet the easy "mere rationality" test. In other words, it just has to be the case that the state is pursuing a legitimate governmental objective, and is doing so with a means that is rationally related to that objective.

Unterscheidung
beeinträchtigen
verfolgen
Möglichkeit

It is very easy for state economic regulation to survive substantive due process attacks. Since 1937, the Court has not struck down an economic regulation for violating substantive due process.

a) Two Requirements

Today, an economic statute has to meet only two easily-satisfied requirements to be in conformity with substantive due process.

- **Legitimate State Objective**: The state must be pursuing a legitimate state objective. But virtually any health, safety or "general welfare" goal comes within the state's "police power" and is thus "legitimate". — Ziel
- **Minimally Rationally Related**: Second, there must be a "minimally rational relation" between the means chosen by the legislature and the state objective. To put it another way, the Court will presume that the statute is constitutional unless the legislature has acted in a completely "arbitrary and irrational" way. — Möglichkeit; willkürlich

b) Other Non-fundamental Rights

Outside the economic area, the same rule applies as long as no fundamental right is being affected: the state must merely be pursuing a legitimate state objective by rational means. So most **"social welfare" legislation merely has to meet this very easy standard**. But what rights are "fundamental"? — In summary, these rights relate to sex, marriage, child-bearing and child-rearing, all components of the general "right to privacy". — Kindererziehung; Recht auf Privatsphäre

For now, the important thing to remember is that if the right does not fall within this grouping of "fundamental" rights, the state must merely act rationally in pursuit of some health, safety or other "general welfare" goal.

2. Fundamental Rights

But if a state or federal government is impairing a "fundamental" right, then it's a different ball game entirely: here, the court uses strict scrutiny. Only if the governmental action is "necessary" to achieve a "compelling" governmental objective, will the government avoid violating substantive due process. — zwingend

III. Enumerated Rights

1. Life

While the Supreme Court has never attempted to define the term life, it has come very close to doing so in its decisions concerning the **prohibition of voluntary abortions**. In *Roe v. Wade* (infra, p. 78) the Court held that the term "person" in the Fourteenth Amendment does not apply to an unborn fetus. The Supreme Court has not dealt with the issue of when a person's life ends following a life birth. — Verbot; Begriff; Fötus

2. Liberty

One may not ascribe a specific meaning to the term "liberty" for it may encompass any form of freedom of action or choice which is accorded constitutional recognition by the Court. — zurückführen

IV. The Right of Privacy and Other Unenumerated Rights

When laws burden the exercise of "fundamental rights" protected by the Due Process guarantee, the courts apply stricter scrutiny. The government bears the burden of showing that the law is narrowly tailored to further an overriding government interest. Often the review is "strict", requiring a showing that the means are "necessary" to a "compelling government interest". — belasten – Ausübung; geschaffen

The rest of the discussion of substantive due process will be solely about fundamental rights, which are governed by the strict scrutiny test.

1. Rights Governed

The only rights that have been recognized as "fundamental" for substantive due process purposes are ones related to the loose category **"right to privacy"**. Sometimes this area is said to involve the **"right to autonomy"** — what is usually meant by this is a person's right to make his own decisions about highly personal matters. This right of privacy or autonomy derives indirectly from several Bill of Rights guarantees, which collectively create a "penumbra" or "zone" of privacy.

Recht auf Selbstbestimmung

persönliche Angelegenheit

herleiten – Grundrechtekatalog

Halbschatten

The list of rights or interests falling within this **"right to privacy"** or **"right to autonomy"** include actually just a few related areas: marriage, child-bearing, and child-rearing. So anytime one is looking at a particularly narrow interest and one is to decide whether it is "fundamental", first one has to ask oneself, "Does it fall within the areas of marriage, child-bearing, or child-rearing?" If not, it is probably not "fundamental".

Kindererziehung

2. Birth Control

Individuals' interest in using birth control is "fundamental". So whether a person is married or single, he or she has a fundamental interest in contraception, and the state cannot impair that interest without satisfying strict scrutiny.

Verhütung

Griswold v. Connecticut – 381 U.S. 479 (1965)

Griswold was the executive director of planned parenthood. He was convicted under a Connecticut statute that made it a crime to assist or counsel someone for the purpose of preventing conception.

geplante Elternschaft

Empfängnis verhindern

Issue

Whether the Connecticut law is a constitutional exercise of the state's police power in view of the substantive due process of the 14th amendment?

Holding and Reasoning

> Lochner v. New York (198 U.S. 45 – 1905) where the Court invalidated the NY law forbidding workers more than 60 hours a week.

The court distanced itself from Lochner, stating that they do not sit as a "super-legislature" to determine the wisdom and need of laws that touch economic or social conditions. However, this law operates directly on the intimate relationship between husband and wife. Although there are rights that are not specifically mentioned in the Bill of Rights, the court has held that they nevertheless are constitutionally protected. For instance the right to choice in education (Pierce v. Society of Sisters, Meyer v. Nebraska). These rights were derived from the 1st amendment right of free speech, which was held to include the freedom of thought and to teach. Without those peripheral rights, the express rights would be less secure. Thus, the 1st amendment has a "penumbra" where "privacy is protected from governmental intrusion". Likewise, the 3rd amendment prohibition against quartering of soldiers, and the 4th amendment prohibition of search and seizure, and the 5th amendment self-incrimination clause, all have a penumbra of privacy. The 9th amendment guarantees that the bill of rights is not to be construed as exclusive of other rights retained by the people. This present case lies within the zone of privacy created by these guarantees.

durch die Verfassung geschützt

Randbereich eines Rechts

einquartieren

Durchsuchung und Beschlagnahme – Selbstbelastung

Dissent Reasoning

> Hugo L. Black (1886-1971)
> Ass. Justice: 1937-1971
> Party: Democrat
> Appointed by: F.D. Roosevelt

[Black] felt that the word "privacy" was being substituted for "liberty", thus he was afraid that the specific guarantees of the bill of rights were being too broadened. The government has a right to invade privacy unless prohibited by some constitutional provision. Broadening these guarantees has the danger of diluting them because the concept of "privacy" can be easily narrowed or

ausweiten

verwässern

broadened according to judicial subjectiveness. The court's analysis here is too much like Lochner in its attempt to find a "natural law" basis for constitutional protections not found in the bill of rights.	Subjektivität Versuch

3. Abortion

The right of abortion is the primary example of a right protected by substantive due process.	Abtreibung

Roe v. Wade – 410 U.S. 113 (1973)

Roe was a single pregnant woman representing a class action suit against a Texas abortion law that made it a crime to "procure an abortion" except "by medical advice for the purpose of saving the life of the mother".	vornehmen lassen

Issue

Whether the Texas anti-abortion law is constitutional.

Majority Reasoning

No. Although the constitution does not explicitly mention the right of privacy, the court has held that it exists. This right is limited to personal rights that are "fundamental". The right of privacy is broad enough to cover a woman's decision to terminate her pregnancy. This right is fundamental but this right is not absolute. Although the fetus is not a "person" under the 14th amendment, a state has an interest in safeguarding health of the mother and in the protection of "potential life". Where there is an attempted regulation of a fundamental right, the state interest must be "compelling". With respect to the interest in the health of the mother, the state's interest becomes "compelling" at the end of the first trimester because it becomes significantly more unsafe to perform an abortion after the first trimester. With respect to the interest in the potential life, the "compelling" point is at the viability of the fetus; when it becomes capable of meaningful life outside the mother's womb - about 7 months. Measured against these standards, the Texas law sweeps too broadly into areas that it does not yet have a "compelling" interest, thus it is an unconstitutional	weit beenden schützen künftiges Leben Unter Berücksichtigung durchführen Lebensfähigkeit – fähig kehren, hineinreichen

invasion of privacy. Thus, the abortion is left to the woman's discretion during the first trimester, it may be regulated in ways that are reasonably related to maternal health after the first trimester and before viability, and may be prohibited after viability.

Eindringen
Ermessen

Dissent Reasoning

> Byron R. White (1917-
> Ass. Justice: 1962-1993
> Party: Democrat
> Appointed by: J. F. Kennedy

[White] The constitution does not guarantee that the mother's right to abortion is absolute before viability. The constitution does not balance the "whim" of the mother who does not have a compelling reason for abortion, over the life of the fetus. The majority's opinion announces this new constitutional right too broadly, removing the state's legislature's power to weigh the impacts of abortion on both sides.
[Rehnquist] There is not a right of "privacy" involved in this case. The right of abortion is not "so rooted in the traditions and conscious of our people as to be ranked fundamental". There is only "liberty" guaranteed by the 14th amendment, which is subject to infringement with due process. The standard should be basic "rational relation". Again, the court goes too far in judging the wisdom of the statute as was the case in Lochner. Breaking the term up into stages and outlining possible regulations that the state may impose on each is usurping the legislative role, not interpreting the 14th amendment.

Laune
mitteilen
wurzeln
Verletzung
umreißen, skizzieren
bemächtigen

But the right of abortion as it stood under Roe v. Wade has been largely overhauled – and cut back – by *Planned Parenthood of Southeastern Pennsylvania v. Casey.* Apparently, abortion is no longer a fundamental right, and restrictions on it are no longer to be strictly scrutinized. This represents a huge departure from the law as it stood under *Roe v. Wade*.

überholen

4. Family Relations

Whenever the state interferes with a person's decision about how to live his **family life and raise his children**, one should be on the lookout to see whether a fundamental right is being interfered with.

groß ziehen

a) Right to Live Together

For instance, relatives have a fundamental right to live together.

Moore v. City of East Cleveland, Ohio – 431 U.S. 494 (1977)

East Cleveland's housing ordinance limited occupancy of a dwelling unit to members of a single family. Part of the ordinance was a strict definition of "family" which excluded Mrs. Inez Moore who lived with her son and two grandsons.

Besetzung, Bewohnen
Wohnung

Issue
Did the housing ordinance violate the Due Process Clause of the Fourteenth Amendment?

Holding and Reasoning
The four justices in the plurality held that the ordinance violated Moore's rights as it constituted "intrusive regulation of the family" without accruing some tangible state interest. Justice Stevens joined in the judgment and argued that the ordinance was invalid because, by regulating who could live with Moore, it constituted a taking of property without just compensation.

aufdringlich
erwachsen

gerechter Ersatz

b) Upbringing and Education

Similarly, a parent's right to direct the upbringing and education of his children is "fundamental".

aa) Right to Continue Parenting

There's also probably a **fundamental right to continue parenting** — so the state cannot take away a child just because it thinks a foster home would be "better" for the child. Even if there's child abuse, the parent still has a fundamental right to parent, but here the state's interest in protecting the child would be "compelling", so putting the child in foster care would probably satisfy strict scrutiny.

Kinderheim
Missbrauch

bb) No Relationship

If a parent has never married the other parent, and has never developed a relationship with the child (e.g., they have never lived together), then there is probably not a fundamental right to continue to be a parent. So the state may, for instance, deny the non-custodial unwed parent who has never participated in the child's upbringing the right to block an adoption of the child.

unverheiratet

c) Right to Marry

The right to marry is also fundamental, so again the state can only interfere with this right by passing strict scrutiny.

5. Adult Sex

There seems to be no general fundamental right to engage in adult consensual sexual activity.

übereinstimmend

a) Homosexual Sodomy

The Supreme Court has struggled with respect to a fundamental right to engage in homosexual sodomy. After not recoguizing a fundamental right in *Bowers v. Hardwick*, a 1986 case, the Supreme Court overruled this case:

Sodomie

Lawrence v. Texas (539 U.S. (2003)

Texan police officers observed Lawrence and another man engaging in a sexual act. Both were arrested and charged an convicted before a Justice of the Peace applying the Texas Penal Code that prohibits "deviate sexual intocourse" between two people of the same sex.

Issue
Whether the Texas Penal Code infringes the Due Process Clause?

Holding and Reasoning
Yes. The court changes its-holding in Bowers. As the laws and traditions have changed in the past half century an "emerging awareness" is obvious that liberty gives substantial protection to adult persons in deciding how to conduct their private lives in matters pertaining to sex. These matters involving the personal diginty and autonomy are protected by the 14th Amendment.

Dissent [Scalia]: Sodomy is not "deeply rooted in the Nation´s history and tradition" and, thus, no fundamental right. Accordingly, the mere rational test is applicable. Prohibiting sodomy is still the majority`s opinion and, thus, a rational basis.

b) Other Sexual Conduct

In fact, outside of the marriage relationship, there is probably no kind of sexual activity the practice of which is a "fundamental right". Thus the state can almost certainly prohibit, and punish, adultery and fornication.

Ehebruch – Unzucht

6. The "Right to Die"

The law of "right to die" and "right to pull the plug" is developing.

den Stecker herausziehen

a) Unwanted Procedures

Nobody can be forced to undergo unwanted procedures. A competent adult has a 14th Amendment liberty interest in not being forced to undergo unwanted medical procedures, including artificial life-sustaining measures. It's not clear whether this is a "fundamental" interest.

The state has an important countervailing interest in preserving life. In the case of a now-incompetent patient, the state's interest in preserving life entitles it to say that it will not allow the "plug" to be "pulled" unless there is "clear and convincing evidence" that the patient would have voluntarily declined the life-sustaining measures.

undergo – sich unterziehen
artificial – künstlich; life-sustaining – lebenserhaltend
countervailing – entgegenstehend
preserving – erhalten
plug – Stecker
declined – ablehnen

b) No "Right to Commit Suicide"

Terminally-ill patients do not have a general liberty interest in "committing suicide". Nor do they have the constitutional right to recruit a third person to help them commit suicide.

interest – Recht
recruit – einstellen, werben

Glucksberg v. Washington, 521 U.S. 702 (1997)

Dr. Harold Glucksberg – along with four other physicians, three terminally ill patients who have since died, and a nonprofit organization that counsels individuals contemplating physician assisted-suicide – brought this suit challenging the state of Washington's ban on physician assisted-suicide. The State of Washington has historically criminalized the promotion of suicide attempts by those who "knowingly cause or aid another person to attempt suicide". Glucksberg alleged that Washington's ban was unconstitutional. Following a District Court ruling favoring Glucksberg and his fellow petitioners, the Ninth Circuit affirmed and the Supreme Court granted Washington certiorari.

assisted-suicide – unterstützter Suizid
ban – Verbot
promotion – Förderung
cause – ermöglichen
petitioners – Antragsteller

Issue

Did Washington's ban on physician assisted-suicide violate the Fourteenth Amendment's Due Process Clause by denying competent terminally ill adults the liberty to choose death over life? — mündig

Holding and Reasoning

No. Analyzing the guarantees of the Due Process Clause, the Court focused on two primary aspects: the protection of the nation's objective fundamental, historically rooted, rights and liberties; and the cautious definition of what constitutes a due process liberty interest. The Court held that the right to assisted suicide is not a fundamental liberty interest protected by the Due Process Clause since its practice has been, and continues to be, offensive to our national traditions and practices. Moreover, employing a rationality test, the Court held that Washington's ban was rationally related to the state's legitimate interest in protecting medical ethics, shielding disabled and terminally ill people from prejudice which might encourage them to end their lives, and, above all, the preservation of human life.

Garantie
wesentlich, wichtig
vorsichtig
anstößig
medizinische Ethik – schützen – Behinderter – Vorurteil
ermutigen

C. Procedural Due Process

I. Introduction

The other aspect of the 14th Amendment's Due Process is the procedural one: this is the requirement that the state act with adequate or fair procedures when it deprives a person of life, liberty or property. Here, the emphasis is on the particular case presented by the particular person — **has the government handled his particular situation fairly**?

Erfordernis
entrechten, nehmen

1. Life, Liberty or Property

The most important single thing to remember about procedural due process is that there cannot be a procedural due process problem unless government is taking a person's life, liberty or property. In other words, there is no general interest in having the government behave with fair procedures.

2. Distinction Between Substance and Procedure

Always distinguish between "substantive" due process and "procedural" due process. Procedural due process applies only where individual determinations are being made.

II. Liberty

"Liberty" is one of the things the government cannot take without procedural due process. What is "liberty" for due process purposes?

1. Physical Liberty

First, there is the interest in "physical" liberty. This liberty interest is violated if one is imprisoned, or even if one is placed in some other situation where he does not have physical freedom of movement (e.g., juvenile and/or civil commitment).

inhaftiert

Bewegungsfreiheit – Jugend-
Begehung

2. Intangible Rights

Also, a person has a liberty interest in being able to do certain intangible things not related to physical freedom of movement. There's no complete catalog of what interests fall within this "intangible" aspect of liberty. Here are some examples, however:

- the right to drive;
- the right to practice one's profession;
- the right to raise one's family.

But one's interest in having a good reputation is not "liberty"

nicht greifbar

groß ziehen
Ruf

Paul v. Davis – 424 U.S. 693 (1976)

A flyer identifying "active shoplifters" was distributed to merchants in the Louisville, Kentucky area. The flyer included a photograph of Edward C. Davis III, who had been arrested on a shoplifting charge. When the charge was dismissed, Davis brought an action against Edgar

Flugblatt – Ladendieb
Kaufleute

Beschuldigung
zurückweisen

Paul, the Louisville chief of police. Davis alleged that the distribution of the flyer had stigmatized him and deprived him of his constitutional rights.

Verteilung – brandmarken – entrechten

Issue

Did the distribution of the flyer violate Davis's right to privacy and liberty under the Due Process Clause of the Fourteenth Amendment?

Holding and Reasoning

In a 5-to-3 decision, the Court held that Davis had not been deprived of any constitutional rights under the Due Process Clause. The Court also emphasized that constitutional privacy interests did not cover Davis's claims. The Court argued that the constitutional right to privacy was limited to matters relating to "marriage, procreation, contraception, family relationships, and child rearing and education". The publication of records of official acts, such as arrests, did not fall under the rubric of privacy rights.

umfassen
Anspruch

Zeugung

III. Property

The government also cannot take "property" without procedural due process. Here are the things that may be "property" for procedural due process purposes:

1. Conventional Property

First, there is "conventional" property (i.e., personal and real property). Thus the government cannot impose a monetary fine against a person, or declare a person's car forfeited, without **complying with procedural due process**.

Unbewegl. Vermögen
Geldstrafe
pfänden – entsprechen

2. Debt Collection

Certain kinds of debt collection devices involve "property". For instance, if the state lets private creditors attach a person's bank account prior to trial (which means that the owner cannot get at the funds), even that temporary blockage is a "taking" of property.

Konto – Prozess
Vermögen

On the other hand, if the state simply passes a law that lets creditors use self-help to repossess goods, there's no governmental taking of property when the creditor repossesses. (The due process requirement applies only where it is government that does, or at least is involved in, the taking of liberty or property).

Selbsthilfe – wiedererlangen

verwickeln

3. Government Benefits

Government benefits may or may not constitute "property" rights. Generally, if one is **just applying** for benefits and has not yet been receiving them, one does **not have a property interest in those benefits**.

Sozialleistung
beantragen
erhalten

But if a person has already been getting the benefits, it's probably the case that he has got a property interest in continuing to get them, so that the government cannot terminate those benefits without giving him procedural due process.

Goldberg v. Kelly, 397 U.S. 254 (1970)

John Kelly, acting on behalf of New York residents receiving financial assistance either under the federally-assisted program for Families with Dependent Children or under New York State's home relief program, challenged the constitutionality of procedures for notice and termination of such aid. Although originally offering no official notice or opportunity for hearings to those whose aid was scheduled for termination, the State of New York implemented a hearing procedure after commencement of Kelly's litigation.

Bewohner

Erleichterung

Möglichkeit

einrichten

Issue

Does a state's termination of public aid, without affording the beneficiary a hearing prior to termination, violate notions of procedural due process as set out in the Fourteenth Amendment's Due Process Clause?

Vorstellung

Holding and Reasoning

Yes. In a 7-to-2 decision, the Court held that states must afford public aid recipients a pre-termination evidentiary

Empfänger – Beweis-

hearing before discontinuing their aid. Noting that welfare benefits are statutory entitlements, rather than "privileges", the Court weighed welfare recipients' need for procedural due process against the competing considerations of the possible harm they might suffer from discontinuation and the government's interest in summary adjudication. The Court concluded that state interests in conserving administrative costs are not sufficient to override public aid recipients' interest in procedural due process. With respect to New York's newly implemented hearings, the Court found them deficient insofar as they did not permit recipients to present evidence, be heard orally in person or through counsel, or cross-examine adverse witnesses.

unterbrechen

abwägen

Überlegung – erleiden

erhalten, bewahren

unzureichend

ins Kreuzverhör nehmen – gegnerisch – Zeuge

IV. Process Required

If a person's interest in property or liberty is being impaired, then he is entitled to due process. But what procedures does the person get? There is no simple answer.

1. Court Proceedings

Where a person is a litigant in a formal judicial proceeding, a large number of procedural safeguards is constitutionally required for "due process". The state is required to give the litigant the right to a hearing, the right to call witnesses, the right to counsel, the right to a fair and objective trial, and the right to an appeal.

Prozessführende Partei
Schutzvorkehrung

Recht, einen Anwalt zu konsultieren – Recht, Rechtsmittel einzulegen

2. Non-judicial Proceeding

Where the property or liberty interest is being impaired in something other than a judicial proceeding, the state does not have to give the individual the full range of procedural safeguards that would be needed for a court proceeding. Instead, for any particular procedural safeguard that the plaintiff says she should get (e.g., the right to a hearing), the court conducts a **balancing test**. The strength of the plaintiff's interest in receiving the procedural safeguard is weighed against the government's interest in avoiding extra burdens.

beeinträchtigen

durchführen

Diagram 15

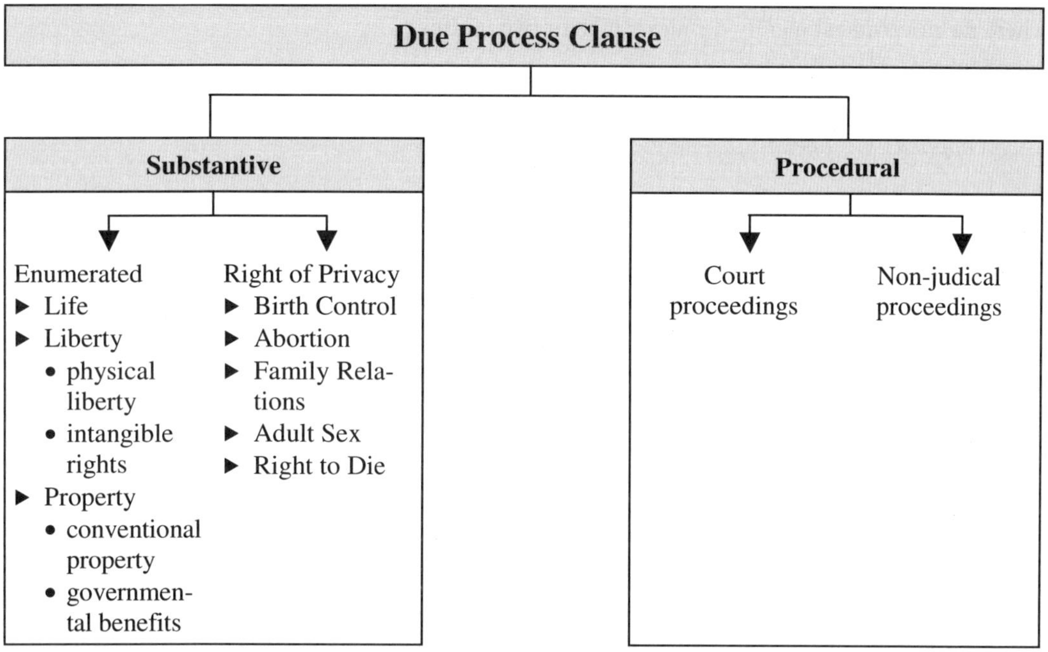

Part 6: Equal Protection

A. Introduction

The Equal Protection Clause of the 14th Amendment has no counterpart in the Constitution applicable to the federal government; it is **limited to state actions**. Nevertheless, it is clear that grossly unreasonable discrimination by the federal government violates the Due Process Clause of the 5th Amendment. Thus, there are **really two equal protection guarantees**. The court applies the same standards under either constitutional provision.

Gegenstück

I. Government Action Only

The Equal Protection Clause, and the Fifth Amendment's Due Process Clause, apply only to government action, not to action by private citizens. This is commonly referred to as the requirement of "state action".

The Equal Protection Clause is only implicated where the government makes a classification. It's not implicated where the government merely decides which of two classes a particular person falls into.

1. "As applied" v. "Facial"

If the plaintiff attacks a classification that is clearly written into the statute or regulation, he is claiming that Equal Protection is violated by the statute or regulation **"on its face"**. If the plaintiff's claim is that the statute does not make a classification on its face, but is being administered in a purposefully discriminatory way, then he is claiming that the statute or regulation is a violation of equal protection **"as applied"**.

Regelung

Either kind of attack – facial or "as applied", may be made. Both follow essentially the same principles. For instance, if no suspect classification or fundamental right is involved, the classification scheme will violate the Equal Protection Clause if it is not rationally related to a legitimate state objective, whether the scheme is on the face of the statute or merely in the way the statute is applied.

2. Clause's Scope

The Clause in essence guarantees that **people who are similarly situated will be treated similarly**.

im Kern

The Equal Protection Clause also guarantees that people who are not similarly situated will not be treated similarly. But this aspect is rarely of practical importance, because courts are rarely convinced that differences in situation require differences in treatment by the government.

überzeugt

II. Three Levels of Review

In the discussion of substantive due process, it was shown that depending on the circumstances, one of two sharply different standards of review of governmental action was used, the easy **"rational relation"** test or the very demanding **"strict scrutiny"** standard. In the Equal Protection context, the two tests are virtually the same as these two, plus a third **"middle level"** of scrutiny.

B. Strict Scrutiny

Strict scrutiny is applied for any classification that involves a "suspect class". There are only three suspect classes generally recognized by the Supreme Court: — "verdächtige Gruppe"

(1) **race**;
(2) **national origin**; and
(3) for some purposes, **alienage**. — Ausländereigenschaft

I. Purposeful

One of the most important things to remember about strict scrutiny of suspect classifications is that this strict scrutiny will only be applied where the differential treatment of the class is intentional on the part of the government and it must be **invidious**. — ungerecht, gemein

1. Purpose

If the government enacts a statute or regulation that merely has the **unintended incidental** effect of burdening, say, African Americans worse than whites, the court will **not use strict scrutiny**. This is probably the most frequently-tested aspect of suspect classifications. However, remember that an intent to classify based on a suspect class can be proven by circumstantial, not just direct, evidence. Here are two contexts in which claims have been made (and in most instances accepted) that a suspect class has been intentionally discriminated against in violation of Equal Protection: — nebensächlich — umstandsbedingt

a) Child Custody and Adoption

Some notion of "racial compatibility" or "racial purity" may motivate state officials to differentiate based on race in child custody and adoption proceedings. In general, the — Bedeutung – Vereinbarkeit practical rule is that the state may not impose flat rules that handle child custody and adoption differently based solely on the race of the child and parents.

Palmore v. Sidoti – 466 U.S. 429 (1984)

A divorced white woman was awarded custody of her child until she remarried a black man. The trial court awarded custody to the father based on the idea that it was in the best interest of the child to protect the child from the discrimination and prejudice that would accompany her remaining with her mother in an interracial family.

zugesprochen

"rassengemischte" Familie

Issue

Whether racial classifications are a constitutional justification for the removal of an infant child from her mother?

Holding and Reasoning

No. Racial classifications trigger strict scrutiny. The classification must be justified by a compelling governmental interest and must be necessary to accomplish a legitimate purpose. Here, the state interest in protecting a child is substantial. It is true that racial discrimination does exist. However, the existence of private prejudices cannot be tolerated by the Constitution, and so are never a justification for racial classifications.

auslösen

schützen

b) Political Process

Actions taken by government that relate to the political process, and that are **intended to disadvantage racial or ethnic minorities**, often run afoul of Equal Protection.

in Kollision stehen

2. Invidious

In addition to the requirement that the discrimination be "purposeful", it must also be "invidious", i.e., based on

gehässig, boshaft

prejudice or tending to denigrate the disfavored class. This requirement is what has caused race, national origin, and (for some purposes) alienage to be the only suspect classes – these involve the only minorities against whom popular prejudice is sufficiently deep.

schlecht machen

II. Race

Classifications based on race or national origin have been held to be suspect, that is, the Justices will use "strict scrutiny" to determine whether the law is invidious. The use of these classifications will be invalid unless they **are necessary to promote a "compelling" interest of government**.

Prior to the Civil War there was no constitutional safeguard against depriving persons of rights and privileges because of their race, the inevitable position of a system which legitimized slavery. But that has changed.

The clearest example of a classification involving a suspect class and thus requiring strict scrutiny is segregation, the maintenance of physical separation between the races. **Official, intentional segregation based on race or national origin is a violation of the Equal Protection Clause**.

Unterhaltung

Brown v. Board of Education of Topeka – 347 U.S. 483 (1954)

Linda Brown was a black child who was denied admission to public schools in her community because of her race. She was not denied access to schools for blacks set up under the "separate but equal" doctrine of *Plessey v. Ferguson*. Class action brought on the behalf of all black students in the U.S.

Plessy v. Ferguson – 163 U.S. 537 (1896): A statute was upheld providing for separate railway carriages for the white and coloured races. The Court held that thistype of separation was constitutional.

Zulassung

Zugang

Issue

Whether the racial classifications in public school admissions are a violation of equal protection, notwithstanding the "separate but equal" doctrine of *Plessey*?

Holding and Reasoning

Yes. There is no conclusive evidence that the framers of the 14th amendment had any idea, or desire, one way or the other to prevent blacks from attending public schools alongside whites. Regardless of whether two separate schools may be called "equal" with respect to the "tangible" factors of buildings, curricula, qualifications of teachers, etc, by definition they cannot be equal with respect to the intangible factors of the ability to take advantage of the environment of the school. In practice, separation of the races promotes the idea of inferiority of the minority race. It generates a feeling of inferiority among the minority race which affects their motivation and eagerness to learn. In public education, separate but equal has no place, and is a denial of equal protection.

schlüssig – Väter

greifbar

nicht greifbar

Unterlegenheit, Minderwertigkeit – erzeugen

Eifer

III. Affirmative Action

In the 1970ies the government started "affirmative actions". That is, that a classification was designed to aid members of racial minorities. In 1989 a majority of the Supreme Court Justices held that **"affirmative action"** also was **subject to strict scrutiny** unless it was narrowly tailored to promote a compelling governmental interest.

Richmond v. J.A. Croson Company – 488 U.S. 469 (1989)

In 1983, the City Council of Richmond, Virginia adopted regulations that required companies awarded city construction contracts to subcontract 30 percent of their business to minority business enterprises. The J.A. Croson Company, which lost its contract because of the 30 percent set-aside, brought suit against the city.

verabschieden

Issue
Did the Richmond law violate the Equal Protection Clause of the Fourteenth Amendment?

Holding and Reasoning
In a 6-to-3 decision, the Court held that "generalized assertions" of past racial discrimination could not justify "rigid" racial quotas for the awarding of public contracts. Justice O'Connor's opinion noted that the 30 percent quota could not be tied to "any injury suffered by anyone", and was an impermissible employment of a suspect classification. O'Connor further held that allowing claims of past discrimination to serve as the basis for racial quotas would actually subvert constitutional values: "The dream of a Nation of equal citizens in a society where race is irrelevant to personal opportunity and achievement would be lost in a mosaic of shifting preferences based on inherently unmeasurable claims of past wrongs."

Behauptung

undurchlässig

zu stürzen versuchen

innewohnend

In 2003 the Supreme Court held that the use of race as a factor in student admissions by universities is constitutional.

Gutter v. Bollinger 539 U.S. 306 (2003)

Gutter applied for admission at the University of Michigan's law school and was rejected because the University pursued a diversity in its student body and, thus, awarding points for blacks, Hispanies and Native Americans. Althrough Gutters's admissions scores were higher access was denied. Gutter sued saying she was victim of illegal discrimination.

Issue
Whether the use of race as a factor in student admissions by a University is unconstitutional?

Holding and Reasoning
No. The Supreme Court held that where the Law School's narrowly tailored use of race in admissions

decisions to further a compelling interest in obtaining the educational benefits that flow from a diverse student body this policy is not prohibited by the Equal Protection Clause.
The Court applies the strict scrutiny test. This test must be used, where there is racial classification by the government. But not all such uses of racial classification are invalidated by strict scrutiny. The Court points out the race-based action necessary to further a compelling governmental interest does not violate the Equal Protection Clause as long as it is narrowly tailored to further that specific interest. When deciding on such action the deciding court must review the context very carefully. The Court makes clear that that student diversity at a university is a compelling interest of the state. Attaining a diverse student body is at the heart of the Law Scholl's proper institutional mission, and its "good faith" is "presumed" absent "a showing to the contrary." On the other side the justices point out that enrolling a "critical mass" of minority students simply to assure some specified percentage of a particular group merely because of its race or ethnic origin would be patently unconstitutional.

IV. Alienage

Alienage might be thought of as a **"semi-suspect"** category. In fact, though, alienage classifications, depending on the circumstances, will be subjected either to strict scrutiny or to mere rationality review.

Ausländereigenschaft

Foley v. Conellie – 435 U.S. 291 (1978)

Edmund Foley applied for a position as a New York state trooper. Although Foley was a legally admitted resident alien, state officials refused to permit him to take the examination. New York authorities relied on a statute providing that "no person shall be appointed to the. . . state police force unless he shall be a citizen of the United States".

bewerben
Polizist
ablehnen

Issue

Did the New York law violate the Equal Protection Clause of the Fourteenth Amendment?

verletzen

Holding and Reasoning

In a 6-to-3 decision, the Court held that the states had an "historical power to exclude aliens from participation in its democratic political institutions" and that the New York statute did not violate the Equal Protection Clause. Noting that states need only to show some rational relationship between a valid state interest and a classification involving aliens, the Court held that the police function was "one of the basic functions of government" and thereby the province of actual United States citizens.

Teilnahme

Beziehung

V. Fundamental Rights

Let's look at the second way strict scrutiny can be triggered in equal protection cases: there will be strict scrutiny not only when a "suspect classification" is used, but also when a "fundamental right" is burdened by the classification the government has selected. Whenever a classification burdens a **"fundamental right"** or "fundamental interest", the classification will be subjected to strict scrutiny even though the people who are burdened are not members of a suspect class.

auslösen

auswählen

unterwerfen, ausgesetzt sein

1. "Fundamental" Defined

"Fundamental" means something absolutely different in this Equal Protection context than it means in the Substantive Due Process context. In due process, the fundamental rights are ones related to privacy. Here, the fundamental rights are related to a variety of other interests protected by the Constitution, but generally having nothing to do with privacy.

Privatheit, Persönlichkeit

2. List

The short list of rights that are "fundamental" for equal protection strict scrutiny purposes is as follows:

(1) the **right to vote**; — Wahlrecht
(2) the right to be a **political candidate**;
(3) the right to have **access to the courts** for certain kinds of proceedings; and — Zugang
(4) the right to **migrate interstate**. — umziehen

VI. Voting Rights

The right to vote in state and local elections is "fundamental", so any classification that burdens that right to vote will be strictly scrutinized.

Harper v. Virginia State Board of Elections – 383 U.S. 663 (1966)

Annie E. Harper, a resident of Virginia, filed suit alleging that the state's poll tax was unconstitutional. After a three-judge district court dismissed the complaint, the case went to the Supreme Court. — Bewohner – behaupten

Issue

Did the Virginia poll tax violate the Equal Protection Clause of the Fourteenth Amendment?

Holding and Reasoning

In a 6-to-3 decision, the Court held that making voter affluence an electoral standard violated the Equal Protection Clause. The Court found that wealth or fee-paying had no relation to voting qualifications. The Court also noted that the Equal Protection Clause was not "shackled to the political theory of a particular era" and that notions of what constituted equal treatment under the Clause were subject to change. — Überfluss; Wohlstand; anketten

VII. Court Access

Access to the courts is sometimes a "fundamental right", so that if the right is burdened by a state-imposed — belasten classification, that classification will sometimes be closely scrutinized. Basically, what it comes down to is that if the state imposes a fee that the rich can pay but the poor cannot, and the access relates to a criminal case, strict scrutiny will be used.

When **civil litigation** is involved, access to the courts is usually **not fundamental**. Only for various family-law proceedings (e.g., divorce, paternity suits, termination of parental rights) is the state barred from charging fees.

Prozessführung

Scheidung – Vaterschaftsklage

hindern

C. Middle Level Review

I. Middle Level Review Generally

A few types of classifications are subjected to "middle-level" review, easier to satisfy than strict scrutiny but tougher than "mere rationality".

There are two main types of classifications that get middle-level review:

(1) **gender**; and

(2) **illegitimacy**.

We also consider alienage here, because it has aspects of both strict scrutiny and mere rationality, so it's kind of a hybrid.

Geschlecht

Unehelichkeit

II. Gender

The most important single rule to remember in the entire area of middle-level scrutiny is that sex-based classifications get **middle-level review**. So if government intentionally classifies on the basis of sex, it has got to show that it is pursuing an important objective, and that the sex-based classification scheme is substantially related to that objective.

verfolgen

1. Benign as well as Invidious

The same standard of review is used whether the sex-based classification is "invidious" (intended to **harm women**) or "benign" (intended to help women, or even intended to **redress past discrimination** against them).

gütig, mild

wiedergutmachen

2. Male or Female Plaintiff

This means that where government classifies based on sex, the scheme can be attacked either by a male or by a female, and either gender will get the benefit of mid-level review.

Craig v. Boren – 429 U.S. 190 (1976)

An Oklahoma statute provides for a minimum age to purchase 3.5% beer differently for males than for females. For females, the age is 18, but for males, the age is 21. The state has statistics that, if valid, tend to show that more males in the 18-20 range than females in the 18- 20 range are arrested for drunk driving. Thus, their rationale for the rule is that it is a necessary protection of public safety.

provides – vorsehen
tend – dazu neigen
drunk driving – Autofahren unter Alkoholeinfluss

Issue

Whether the law violates the equal protection clause, i.e. whether the difference between males and females with respect to the purchase of 3.2% beer does not justify the differential treatment by the Oklahoma statute.

Holding Reasoning

Yes. Reed and Fornteiro stand for the proposition that classification by gender must serve "important governmental objectives" and must be "substantially related" to the achievement of those objectives. The purpose of increasing traffic safety is certainly "important" and valid. However, the relationship between the classification and the objective is not sufficiently "substantial". The statistical evidence presented is statistically invalid because it rests on too many assumptions which have not been proven. Also, even given their correctness, they do not justify differential treatment because of their close results. There is an inherent difficulty (i.e. too many uncontrollable variables) in using statistical evidence to make broad social classifications.

achievement – objectives: Erreichen – Ziele
invalid – unwirksam
assumptions – Annahme
uncontrollable – unkontrolliert

Sex-based classifications will only be subjected to middle-level review if the legislature has intentionally discriminated against one sex in favor of the other. If, as the result of some governmental act, one sex happens to suffer an unintended burden greater than the other sex suffers, that's not enough for mid-level review.

3. Stereotypes

Be on the lookout for stereotypes: if the legislature has made a sex-based classification that seems to reinforce **stereotypes about the "proper place" of women**, it probably cannot survive middle-level review.

verstärken

U.S. v. Virginia, 518 U.S. 515 (1996)

The Virginia Military Institute (VMI) boasted a long and proud tradition as Virginia's only exclusively male public undergraduate higher learning institution. The United States brought suit against Virginia and VMI alleging that the school's male-only admissions policy was unconstitutional insofar as it violated the Fourteenth Amendment's equal protection clause. On appeal from a District Court ruling favoring VMI, the Fourth Circuit reversed. It found VMI's admissions policy to be unconstitutional. Virginia, in response to the Fourth Circuit's reversal, proposed to create the Virginia Women's Institute for Leadership (VWIL) as a parallel program for women. On appeal from the District Court's affirmation of the plan, the Fourth Circuit ruled that despite the difference in prestige between the VMI and VWIL, the two programs would offer "substantively comparable" educational benefits. The United States appealed to the Supreme Court.

sich rühmen

Zulassungskriterium

aufheben

vorschlagen

Berufung einlegen

Issue

Does Virginia's creation of a women's-only academy, as a comparable program to a male-only academy, satisfy the Fourteenth Amendment's Equal Protection Clause?

Holding and Reasoning

No. In a 7-to-1 decision, the Court held that VMI's male-only admissions policy was unconstitutional. Because it failed to show "exceedingly persuasive justification" for VMI's gender-biased admissions policy, Virginia violated the Fourteenth Amendment's equal protection clause. Virginia failed to support its claim that single-sex education contributes to educational diversity because it did not show that VMI's male-only admissions policy was created or maintained in order to further educational diversity. Furthermore, Virginia's VWIL could not offer women the same benefits as VMI offered men. The VWIL would not provide women with the same rigorous military training, faculty, courses, facilities, financial opportunities, or alumni reputation and connections that VMI affords its male cadets.

Finally, the Fourth Circuit's "substantive comparability" between VMI and VWIL was misplaced. The Court held that the Fourth Circuit's "substantive comparability" standard was a displacement of the Court's more exacting standard, requiring that "all gender-based classifications today" be evaluated with "heightened scrutiny". When evaluated with such "heightened scrutiny", Virginia's plan to create the VWIL would not provide women with the same opportunities as VMI provides its men and so it failed to meet requirements of the equal protection clause.

gender-biased: geschlechtsdiskriminierend
diversity: Verschiedenheit
maintained: unterhalten
rigorous: streng
alumni reputation: Ansehen der Ehemaligen
cadets: Kadett

III. Illegitimacy

Miller v. Albright – 523 U.S. 420 (1998)

Lorelyn Miller was born in the Philippines, in 1970, to a Filipino national woman and an American soldier. Her parents were never married. In 1992, after the State Department rejected her first application for U.S. citizenship, Miller reapplied when a Texas court granted her father's petition for a paternity decree declaring him her father. When the State Department rejected her citizenship application again, claiming that 8 U.S.C.

paternity: Vaterschaft

§1409(a) required foreign born illegitimate children of American fathers to be legitimated before age 18, Miller challenged the refusal. She claimed that since §1409(c) established at birth the citizenship of an illegitimate foreign-born child whose mother was an American citizen, the State Department's refusal to do the same under §1409(a), when the father is an American citizen, was unconstitutional. On appeal from an appellate court's decision to affirm the lower court's dismissal of the case, the Supreme Court granted Miller certiorari.

Ablehnung

verfassungswidrig

Issue

Does 8 U.S.C. §1409, establishing upon birth the U.S. citizenship of illegitimate foreign-born children whose mothers only are U.S. citizens but failing to do the same if only their fathers are U.S. citizens, violate the Fifth Amendment's equal protection guarantees?

unterlassen

Holding and Reasoning

No. After ruling that Miller had standing to challenge the constitutionality of a federal statute, the Court held that 8 U.S.C. §1409 did not violate the Equal Protection Clause. The Court reasoned that different treatment of mothers and fathers of out-of-wedlock children was justified since the two parents are not "similarly situated". While the child's relationship with its father may be undisclosed for several years, its blood relationship to its mother is usually apparent through hospital records. Moreover, whereas birth mothers will know immediately of their child's existence, birth fathers and their children may never know each other. The statutory requirement that a child born out of wedlock to a citizen father obtain formal proof of paternity by age 18, either through legitimization, written acknowledgment by the father under oath, or adjudication by a competent court, is well tailored to address the difficulties of establishing a child's citizenship based only on the relation to the father.

Bundesgesetz

unehelich geboren

unentdeckt

offenkundig - Akten

Erfordernis

Vaterschaft

Eid – zuständiges Gericht

D. The "Mere Rationality" Test

I. Non-suspect, Non-fundamental Rights

First, the treatment of classifications shall be examined that do not involve either a suspect class or a fundamental right. Most economic and social-welfare legislation falls into this category.

Sozial-

1. Mere Rationality

Here, as noted, courts use the "mere rationality" standard. In other words, as long as there is **some rational relation** between the classification drawn by the legislature and some legitimate legislative objective, the classification scheme will not violate the Equal Protection Clause.

legitimes gesetzliches Ziel

a) Need Not be Actual Objective

One thing this "mere rationality" standard means is that the "legitimate government objective" part of the test is satisfied even if the statute's defenders come up with merely a "hypothetical" objective that the legislature "might have" been pursuing. The government does not have to show that the objective it is pointing to was the one that actually motivated the legislature.

Verteidiger
hypothetisch
verfolgen

b) No Empirical Link

Also, there does not have to in fact be even a "rational relation" between the means chosen and the end — all that's required is that the **legislature "could have rationally believed"** that there was a link between the means and the end.

Möglichkeit – Ziel

2. Non-suspect Classes

Here is a partial list of classifications that have been held not to involve a suspect or quasi-suspect class:

"halbverdächtig"

a) Age

Age is not a suspect class. Thus, government's actions based on age will be upheld if there is a **conceivable rational basis for the classification**. — denkbar

Massachusetts Board of Retirement v. Murgia – 427 U.S. 307 (1976)

Massachusetts had a law that provided for mandatory retirement of police officers upon reaching age 50. The stated purpose was the protection of the public by assuring that police officers are physically fit. — zwingend; Pension

Issue

Whether classification of police officers by age is a violation of the equal protection clause.

Holding and Reasoning

No. Age is not a suspect classification for police officers, and so strict scrutiny is not triggered. Thus, the more relaxed rational basis test will be applied. Classification by age is not perfect in deciding who is physically fit to be a police officer, but perfection is not required. Age bears a rational relationship to fitness, and so the law is valid. The fact that the state does not use individual testing instead of an across-the-board mandatory retirement does not make the law irrational, only imperfect. — auslösen; nicht erforderlich; tragen; zwingend

b) Mental Condition

Classifications based upon mental illness or mental retardation are not a suspect class either.

City of Cleburne, Texas v. Cleburne Living Center – 473 U.S. 432 (1985)

A Texas city denied a special use permit to a person who intended to build a 200-person home for the mentally retarded. A city ordinance gave the city the power to — geisteskrank require a special use permit for homes for mentally retarded persons, but not for other classifications, such as sanitariums, nursing homes, etc. The city's rationale was that the neighboring property owners did not want it, a junior high school was across the street, it was located on a 500 year flood plain, and there would be a lot of people living there.

Pflegeheim

Überschwemmung

Issue

Whether the ordinance requiring a special use permit hearing for establishment of mentally retarded care homes violates equal protection, and under what standard.

Majority Reasoning

[White] Yes. The general rule for equal protection is rational basis. The mentally retarded are not a class that require heightened scrutiny because they are

- not a homogenous group,
- they are specially protected in many ways by the legislature, and
- most laws concerning the mentally retarded are likely to be beneficial and not based on prejudice.

homogen

Gesetzgeber

vorteilhaft – Vorurteil

However, here the law appears to be motivated only by prejudice. The negative attitudes of the surrounding property owners are not a valid basis for discrimination. Also, there are no other distinguishing characteristics that are inherent to the retarded people that would require that they be treated differently with regard to the location of the home, or its size. Clearly, if other homes, such as those for the insane, or convalescent, are allowed in the same area, the law is not even rationally related to the city's objectives because it is substantially underinclusive.

Kranke – Genesende

c) Sexual Orientation

Regarding classifications based on sexual orientation, states face only mere-rationality review if they treat homosexuals differently from heterosexuals.

But the Court now seems to review anti-gay legislation a bit more skeptically than most legislation not involving a semi-suspect or suspect class, even though gays still do not have suspect or semi-suspect status.

Diagram 16

Amendment XIV. (1868)

Section. 1. All persons born or naturalized in the United States and subject to the jurisdiction thereof, are citizens of the United States and of the State wherein they reside. No State shall make or enforce any law which shall abridge the privileges or immunities of citizens of the United States; nor shall any State deprive any person of life, liberty, or property, without due process of law; n**or deny to any person within its jurisdiction the equal protection of the laws**.

Strict Scrutiny	**Middle Level**	**Mere Rationality**
▶ Race (Brown v. Board of Education) ▶ National origin ▶ Fundamental Rights • Right to vote • Right to be a political candidate • Court access • Right to migrate inter-state	▶ Gender • both benign and in-vidious • stereotypes (U.S. v. Virginia) ▶ Illegitimacy	▶ Age ▶ Mental condition ▶ Sexual orientation
law will be upheld only if it is necessary to achieve a **compelling and overriding government pupose**	law will be upheld of it is substantially related to an **important government pupose**	law will be upheld of it is rationally related to a **legimate interest**

Part 7: Freedom of Expression

A. Introduction

The First Amendment provides, in part, that

> *"Congress shall make no law...abridging the freedom of speech, or of the press; or the right of the people peaceably to assemble, and to petition the Government for a redress of grievances".*

Whenever one considers governmental action that seems to infringe upon the freedom of expression, there is one key question that one must always ask before one asks anything else. That question is, "Is this governmental action 'content-based' or 'content-neutral'?" If the action is "content-based", the government's action will generally be subjected to strict scrutiny, and the action will rarely be sustained. On the other hand, if the action is "content-neutral", the government's action is subjected to a much less demanding standard, and is thus much more likely to be upheld.

inhaltswertend – inhaltsneutral

B. Analysis of Content-based Government Action

Once it is determined that a particular government action impairing expression is "content-based", one then has to determine whether the expression falls within a category that is protected by the First Amendment.

I. Unprotected Category

If the speech falls into certain pre-defined unprotected categories, then the government can basically ban that expression completely based on its content, without any interference at all from the First Amendment.
The main "unprotected" categories are:

vordefiniert – ungeschützt

- obscenity
- fraudulent misrepresentation;
- defamation;

Obszönität
betrügerische Falschdarstellung
Verleumdung

- advocacy of imminent lawless behavior; and
- "fighting words".

But even speech falling within an "unprotected category" receives one small First Amendment protection: **government must regulate in a basically content-neutral way**.

R.A.V. v. City of St. Paul, Minnesota – 505 U.S. 377 (1992)

Several teenagers allegedly burned a crudely fashioned cross on a black family's lawn. The police charged one of the teens under a local bias-motivated criminal ordinance which prohibits the display of a symbol which "arouses anger, alarm or resentment in others on the basis of race, color, creed, religion or gender". The trial court dismissed this charge. The state supreme court reversed. R.A.V. appealed to the U.S. Supreme Court.

roh

durch Vorurteil geprägt – Satzung – hervorrufen
Zorn
Konfession – abweisen
aufheben
Berufung einlegen

Issue
Is the ordinance overly broad and impermissibly content-based in violation of the First Amendment free speech clause?

Holding and Reasoning
Yes. In a 9-to-0 vote, the justices held the ordinance invalid on its face because "it prohibits otherwise permitted speech solely on the basis of the subjects the speech addresses". The First Amendment prevents government from punishing speech and expressive conduct because it disapproves of the ideas expressed. Under the ordinance, for example, one could hold up a sign declaring that all anti-Catholic bigots are misbegotten; but not that all papists are, for that would insult and provoke violence on the basis of religion. Government has no authority "to license one side of a debate to fight freestyle, while requiring the other to follow the Marquis of Queensbury Rules".

missbilligen

Frömmler
Papisten
verletzen

Eighth Marquis of Queensbury (1844–1900)
British aristocrat and boxing promoter who formulated the Marquis of Queensbury Rules (1867) to govern boxing.

1. Obscenity

Miller v. California – 413 U.S. 15 (1973)

Miller, after conducting a mass mailing campaign to advertise the sale of "adult" material, was convicted of violating a California statute prohibiting the distribution of obscene material. Some unwilling recipients of Miller's brochures complained to the police, initiating the legal proceedings.

werben
vertreiben
Empfänger

Issue
Is the sale and distribution of obscene materials by mail protected under the First Amendment's freedom of speech guarantee?

Holding and Reasoning
In a 5-to-4 decision, the Court held that obscene materials did not enjoy First Amendment protection. The Court modified the test for obscenity established in Roth v. United States and Memoirs v. Massachusetts, holding that "[t]he basic guidelines for the trier of fact must be: (a) whether 'the average person, applying contemporary community standards' would find that the work, taken as a whole, appeals to the prurient interest. . . (b) whether the work depicts or describes, in a patently offensive way, sexual conduct specifically defined by the applicable state law; and (c) whether the work, taken as a whole, lacks serious literary, artistic, political, or scientific value". The Court rejected the "utterly without redeeming social value" test of the Memoirs decision.

genießen
Tatsacheninstanz
anwendbar

2. Fighting Words

"Fighting words" are words which are likely to make the person to whom they are addressed commit an act of violence, probably against the speaker. Expression that falls within the "fighting words" category can be flatly banned or punished by the state.

kategorisch

Chaplinsky v. State of New Hampshire – 315 U.S. 568 (1941)

Chaplinsky, a Jehovah's Witness, called a city marshal a "God-damned racketeer" and "a damned fascist" in a public place. He was arrested and convicted under a state law for violating a breach of the peace.

Gauner

Issue

Does the application of the statute violate Chaplinsky's freedom of speech protected by the First Amendment?

Anwendung
geschützt

Holding and Reasoning

No. Some forms of expression--among them obscenity and fighting words--do not convey ideas and thus are not subject to First Amendment protection. In this case, Chaplinsky uttered fighting words, i.e., words that "inflict injury or tend to incite an immediate breach of the peace".

überbringen
sofortig

II. Protected Category

All expression not falling into one of these five pre-defined categories is "protected". If expression is protected, then any government ban or restriction on it based on its content will be presumed to be unconstitutional.

Inhalt
annehmen

C. Analyzing Content-neutral Regulations

If the government restriction is content-neutral, there is a **three-part** test that the government must satisfy before its regulation will be sustained if that regulation substantially impairs expression:

Regeln – aufrechterhalten
beeinträchtigen

- **Significant governmental interest**: First, the regulation must serve a significant governmental interest.
- **Narrowly tailored**: Second, the regulation must be narrowly tailored to serve that governmental interest. So if there's a somewhat less restrictive way to accomplish the same result, the government must use that less-intrusive way.

zuschneiden
weniger aufdringlich

- **Alternative channels**: Finally, the state must "leave open alternative channels" for communicating the information.

Now, the focus is on regulations covering the "time, place and manner" of expression. The rules for analyzing "time, place and manner" restrictions only apply if the speech that is being restricted is taking place in a public forum.
Many cases arose because of governmental attempts to require a **license or permit before expressive conduct takes place**. The licensing scheme must set forth the grounds for denying a permit narrowly and specifically, so that the discretion of local officials will be curtailed.

betreffen
Öffentlichkeit
entstehen
Lizenz
Zulassung
Ermessen – kürzen

City of Lakewood v. Plain Dealer Pub. Co. – 486 U.S. 750 (1988)

Plain Dealer Publishing challenged the constitutionality of a Lakewood city ordinance that authorized its mayor to grant or deny applications, made by publishers, seeking permission to place newsracks on public property. The ordinance merely required Lakewood's mayor to provide an explanation, in the event of a permit denial, while empowering him to subject all permit approvals to whatever "terms and conditions" which he "deemed necessary and reasonable". On appeal from a district court ruling that found the ordinance constitutional, the Court of Appeals reversed. The Supreme Court granted Lakewood's request for certiorari.

angreifen
Verleger
Zeitungsstand – öffentlicher Platz
ermächtigen

Issue
Did Lakewood's city ordinance violate freedom of speech rights as protected by the First Amendment?

Holding and Reasoning
Yes. The Court held that the licensing ordinance was facially invalid since it gave Lakewood's mayor unbridled discretion to discriminate against permit seekers, based on the content of their publications and viewpoints. This, in turn, promoted self-censorship by

zügellos – Antragsteller
Standpunkt – Selbstzensur

publishers and other speakers who sought to curry favor with the mayor's officer in order to secure the approval of their licensing requests. The Court added that while cities may require the periodic licensing of newsracks on public property, even subjecting such procedures to reasonable restrictions, they may not use language which is so open-ended as to give city officials unlimited subjective discretion over permit approvals.

sich bei jmd. lieb Kind machen

unbegrenzt

Ermessen

Diagram 17

Freedom of Expression

– Amendment I. (1791) –

Congress shall make no law respecting an establishment of religion, or prohibiting the free exercise thereof; or *abridging the freedom of speech*, or of the press; or the right of the people peaceably to assemble, and to petition the Government for a redress of grievances.

content based

- ▶ unprotected
  - obscenity
  - fraudulent misrepresentant
  - defamation
  - fighting words
- ▶ protected
  other kinds of catergories are protected –> thus, any government ban or restriction is presumed to be unconstitutional

content neutral

- ▶ 3-Part-Test
  - significant government interest
  - regulation is narrowly tailored
  - alternativ channels must be left open

D. Symbolic Expressions

"Symbolic expression" is an expression that consists solely of **non-verbal actions**.

I. Introduction

Essentially the same rules are used to analyze restrictions on symbolic expression as for restrictions that apply to verbal speech, or to verbal speech coupled with conduct. Thus: — verbinden

(1) any attempt by government to restrict symbolic expression because of the content of the message will be **strictly scrutinized** and almost certainly struck down;

(2) any restriction on the **time, place or manner** of symbolic expression will have to be narrowly tailored to a significant governmental objective and will have to leave open alternative channels.

II. Flag Desecration

The most interesting example of government regulation of symbolic expression is flag desecration statutes. The main thing to remember is that **if a statute bans flag desecration or mutilation**, and either on the statute's face or as it is applied, the **statute is directed only at particular messages, it will be invalid**.

Entweihung
Verstümmelung

Eichman v. US – 496 U.S. 310 (1990)

In 1989, Congress passed the Flag Protection Act which made it a crime to destroy an American flag or any likeness of an American flag which may be "commonly displayed". The law did, however, allow proper disposal of a worn or soiled flag. Several prosecutions resulted from the Act. Eichman set a flag ablaze on the steps of the U.S. Capitol while protesting the government's domestic and foreign policy. Another prosecution (*United States v.*

abgenutzt – schmutzig
entflammen

Haggerty) resulted from a flag-burning in Seattle protesting the passage of the Flag Protection Act. Both cases (*Eichman's* and *Haggerty's*) were argued together. — Flaggenverbrennung

Issue

Did the Act violate freedom of expression protected by the First Amendment?

Holding and Reasoning

Yes. In a 5-to-4 decision, coming on the heels of a similar holding in *Texas v. Johnson* (1989), the Court struck down the law because "its asserted interest is related to the suppression of free expression and concerned with the content of such expression". Allowing the flag to be burned in a disposal ceremony but prohibiting protestors from setting it ablaze at a political protest made that clear, argued Justice Brennan in one of his final opinions.

Ferse
behaupten
Zerstörungszeremonie

William J. Brennan (1906-1997)
Ass. Justice: 1956-1990
Party: Democrat
Nominated by: Eisenhower

E. Commercial Speech

I. Introduction

Speech that is "commercial" – that is, speech advertising a product or proposing some commercial transaction – gets **First Amendment protection**. But this protection is in some ways more limited than the protection given to non-commercial (e.g., political) speech.

werben
vorstellen

1. Truthful Speech

Truthful commercial speech gets a pretty fair degree of First Amendment protection. The government may restrict truthful commercial speech only if the regulation

ehrlich

- directly advances

fördern

- a substantial governmental interest
- in a way that is "no more extensive than necessary" to achieve the government's objective.

Virginia Pharmacy Board v. Virginia Consumer Council – 425 U.S. 748 (1976)

Acting on behalf of prescription drug consumers, the Virginia Citizens Consumer Council challenged a Virginia statute that declared it unprofessional conduct for licensed pharmacists to advertise their prescription drug prices. On appeal from an adverse ruling by a three-judge District Court panel, the Supreme Court granted the Virginia State Board of Pharmacy review.

Rezept

unprofessionelles Verhalten

Überprüfung

Issue

Is a statutory ban on advertising prescription drug prices by licensed pharmacists a violation of "commercial speech" under the First Amendment?

Verbot

Holding and Reasoning

Yes. In a 7-to-1 opinion, the Court held that the First Amendment protects willing speakers and willing listeners equally. The Court noted that in cases of commercial speech, such as price advertising, freedom of speech protections apply just as they would to noncommercial speech. Even speech that is sold for profit, or involves financial solicitations, is protected. The Court concluded that although the Virginia State Board of Pharmacy has a legitimate interest in preserving professionalism among its members, it may not do so at the expense of public knowledge about lawful competitive pricing terms.

bereit

Hilfe

bewahren

2. False, Deceptive or Illegal

On the other hand, false or deceptive commercial speech **may be forbidden by the government**. Similarly, speech which proposes an illegal transaction may be forbidden (e.g., advertisements for cocaine).

täuschend

If the product or service is harmful but lawful, the state may forbid or limit advertising about the product so long as it could completely ban the product.

Posadas de Puerto Rico Assoc. v. Tourism Co. of Puerto Rico – 478 U.S. 328 (1986)

> Status of Puerto Rico: Self governing entity in association with the U.S. An elected resident Commissioner sits in the U.S. House of Representatives but cannot vote. Puerto Ricans share all the rights and obligations of the U.S. citizenship, including service in the armed forces; however, they do not pay federal taxes and cannot vote in national elections.

A Puerto Rican law restricted advertising by the island's casino gambling establishments. Even though gambling was a legal activity in Puerto Rico, the law only allowed advertising that was targeted at tourists.

spielen

richten auf

Issue

Did the law violate the First Amendment?

Holding and Reasoning

No. The Court held that the Act passed the constitutional test for restrictions on commercial speech. Justice Rehnquist argued that Puerto Rico's desire to protect the "health, safety, and welfare of its citizens" by attempting to isolate them from casino advertising served a "substantial government interest". The law was clearly drawn and directly related to the government's goal of minimizing the ill effects, such as prostitution and crime, that gambling cultivates in local communities.

minimieren – Prostitution

erhalten

Part 8: Freedom of Religion

A. First Amendment Religious Freedoms

There are two "religion clauses" of the First Amendment. One guarantees a right to the **"free exercise"** of religion, while the other prohibits any "law respecting the **establishment of religion**". A factor making it difficult to apply these clauses is the fact that the Framers had divergent views as to what the religion clauses meant.

freie Ausübung

Errichtung einer Religion

Verfassungsväter

Another complicating factor in applying the religion clauses is that the "free exercise" clause and the "establishment" clause are ultimately contradictory. — widersprüchlich

I. The Establishment Clause

The test of whether a law or practice has the required neutrality toward religion is determined according **a three-part test** developed in Lemon v. Kurtzman:

Lemon v. Kurtzman – 403 U.S. 602 (1971)

This case was heard concurrently with two others, *Early v. DiCenso* (1971) and *Robinson v. DiCenso* (1971). The cases involved controversies over laws in Pennsylvania and Rhode Island. In Pennsylvania, a statute provided financial support for teacher salaries, textbooks, and instructional materials for secular subjects to non-public schools. The Rhode Island statute provided direct supplemental salary payments to teachers in non-public elementary schools. Each statute made aid available to "church-related educational institutions".

Gehalt
weltlich

Issue

Did the Rhode Island and Pennsylvania statutes violate the First Amendment's Establishment Clause by making state financial aid available to "church-related educational institutions"?

Holding and Reasoning

Warren E. Burger (1907-1995)
Chief Justice: 1969-1986
Party: Republican
Nominated by: R. Nixon

Yes. Writing for the majority, Chief Justice Burger arti-culated a three-part test for laws dealing with religious establishment. To be constitutional, a statute must have "a secular legislative purpose", it must have principal effects which neither advance nor inhibit religion, and it must not foster "an excessive government entanglement with religion". The Court found that the subsidization of parochial schools furthered a process of religious inculcation, and that the "continuing state surveillance" necessary to enforce the specific provisions of the laws would inevitably entangle the state in religious affairs. The Court also noted the

weltlich
verbieten
hegen – Verbindung
Unterstützung
kirchlich
Einschärfung – Überwachung

verbinden

presence of an unhealthy "divisive political potential" concerning legislation which appropriates support to religious schools.

Thus three criteria must be fulfilled to determine a law's religious neutrality:

- statute must have a secular **legislative purpose** — weltlich
- principal effects **neither advance nor inhibit religion**
- statute must not foster an **excessive government entanglement with religion**

II. School Cases

By far, the greatest number of establishment clause issues that have arisen have involved the nexus of religion and the schools. This has two aspects. First, since the **public school system in the United States is run by the government**, it may not use it to "establish" any particular religion or even to encourage religion in general. Second, there is a healthy system of private schools responsible for the education of a substantial minority of children in the country. Many of these schools are run by religious institutions. To the extent that the government assists those schools in teaching children, it can be accused of aiding that religion.

aufkommen
ermutigen
Zu dem Ausmaß
beschuldigen

1. Religion in Public Schools

While public school students may be required to study religion or the Bible as part of a secular program on that subject, **a public school may not require religious exercises in class**. It does not matter whether the exercises are denominational or non-denominational. Even a period of silence for "meditation or voluntary prayer" is prohibited, at least when it is implemented in order to "return voluntary prayer to the public schools".

konfessionell

Excusing objecting children from such activities is not a solution. In fact, excluding students exacerbates the problem, since the objecting students' relationship with their classmates and teacher may be affected, and the effect would be based on religious differences.

widersprechende
verschlimmern

Stone v. Graham – 449 U.S. 39 (1980)

Sydell Stone and a number of other parents challenged a Kentucky state law that required the posting of a copy of the Ten Commandments in each public school classroom. They filed a claim against James Graham, the super–intendent of public schools in Kentucky.

aufhängen
10 Gebote

Issue

Did the Kentucky statute violate the Establishment Clause of the First Amendment?

Holding and Reasoning

Yes. In a 5-to-4 per curiam decision, the Court ruled that the Kentucky law violated the first part of the test established in Lemon v. Kurtzman, and thus violated the Establishment Clause of the Constitution. The Court found that the requirement that the Ten Commandments be posted "had no secular legislative purpose" and was "plainly religious in nature". The Court noted that the Commandments did not confine themselves to arguably secular matters (such as murder, stealing, etc.), but rather concerned matters such as the worship of God and the observance of the Sabbath Day.

begrenzen
Anbetung
Beachtung

2. Pledge of Allegiance

Many US schools start their day with the Pledge of Allegiance including the phrase "one nation under God":

Elk Grove Unified School District v. Newdow (328 F 3d 466-2004)

Michael Newdow's daughter was reguired to recite the Pledge of Allegiance in school every morning. He challenged the word "under God".

Issue
Whether the Pledge of Allegiance infringes the 1st Amendment?

Holding and Reasoning
No. The phrase "under God" is a declaration of belief in allegiance and loyality to the USA. It is in no sense a prayer, nor an endorsement of any religion, but a simple recognition that from time of our earliest history our peoples and institutions have reflected the traditional concept that our nation was founded an a fundamental belief in God

3. Financial Assistance to Religious Schools

Cases dealing with governmental assistance to religious schools (also called **"parochial" schools**) are numerous as well. Many of the decisions in this area are contradictory, as members of the Court sharply divide on the proper approach and recent changes in personnel on the Court complicate matters. The requisite neutrality under the Lemon test was found in state programs that provided reimbursement to parents for the expense of public bus transportation to private schools, loans of state-approved secular textbooks to children in religious schools, and state funding of state-required standardized tests. However, the Court disapproved state salary supplements for private (including religious) school teachers of secular subjects.

widersprüchlich

Ansatz

komplizieren

Auszahlung

III. Other Establishment Clause Issues

Government **recognition of religious holidays** has been permitted as satisfying the Lemon test's second requirement that government action be supported by a secular purpose. Common in some parts of the United States are **"blue laws"**, which require that businesses be closed on Sundays. These laws were originally based on Sunday being the day of worship for Christians and a "day of rest".

Anerkennung

Gesetz zum Schutz des Sonntags

McGowan v. State of Maryland – 366 U.S. 420 (1961)

Several employees of a discount department store sold a few items, such as floor wax and loose-leaf notebooks, to customers on a Sunday. By doing so, they violated Maryland's blue laws which only allow certain items, such as drugs, tobacco, newspapers and some foodstuffs, to be sold on Sundays.

Angestellte
Notizblöcke

Issue
Do Maryland's blue laws violate the Free Exercise and Religious Establishment clauses of the First Amendment?

Holding and Reasoning
No. The Court found that the blue laws did not violate the Free Exercise Clause because the employees allege only economic injury and not infringement on their own religious practices. The Court also found that the blue laws did not violate the division between church and state. Sunday closing laws started out to facilitate church attendance in colonial America; however, the present Maryland laws are based on secular rather than religious state interests. The laws are to improve the "health, safety, recreation, and general well-being" of citizens. The present purpose of the laws is to provide a uniform day of rest for all. The fact that this day is of particular significance for various Christian sects does not bar the State from achieving its secular goals.

behaupten
Verletzung
Anwesenheit
Erholung
Sekten

Secular purpose also justifies government recognition of Christmas, the most important holiday of the year in the United States for most people. As the Court has noted, despite its religious origins, **Christmas is really observed as a holiday of gift-giving and other secular activities**. However, the government may not "endorse" the original Christian religious significance of Christmas by way of public display of a nativity scene of Jesus' birth on public property.

Feiertag
Schenken
billigen
Geburtsszene

Allegheny County v. American Civil Liberties Union – 492 U.S. 573 (1989)

Two public-sponsored holiday displays in Pittsburgh, Pennsylvania, were challenged by the American Civil Liberties Union. The first display involved a Christian nativity scene inside the Allegheny County Courthouse. The second display was a large Chanukah menorah, erected each year by the Chabad Jewish organization, outside the City-County building. The ACLU claimed the displays constituted state endorsement of religion.

sich beziehen auf

errichten

Issue

Did the public displays violate the Establishment Clause of the First Amendment?

Holding and Reasoning

In a 5-to-4 decision, the Court held that the crèche inside the courthouse unmistakably endorsed Christianity in violation of the Establishment Clause. By prominently displaying the words "Glory to God for the birth of Jesus Christ", the county sent a clear message that it supported and promoted Christian orthodoxy. The Court also held, however, that not all religious celebrations on government property violated the Establishment Clause. Six of the justices concluded that the display involving the menorah was constitutionally legitimate given its "particular physical setting".

Krippe

unterstützen

fördern

B. The Free Exercise Clause

The paradigm violation of the free exercise clause is when the government acts to disadvantage people because of their religion. Laws that do this explicitly are rare. Most free exercise claims instead involve laws that pursue some **permissible public purpose**, but which allegedly burden religious beliefs indirectly. What the challenger seeks is an exemption from a general law.

Musterbeispiel

benachteiligen

statthaft

I. Traditional vs. New Free Exercise Standards

For years, the Court applied a strict scrutiny test under which it would first determine whether the burden on religious beliefs was significant and, if it was, would sustain the law only if it was narrowly drawn to achieve a compelling state interest. In determining the question, the availability of less restrictive alternatives was to be considered.

bestimmen
erreichen – zwingend
Verfügbarkeit

However, in the recent case of Employment Division, Department of Human Resources v. Smith, the Court announced that it will no longer follow this process of balancing the burden on religion against a compelling state interest. Instead, so long as the purpose of the law is not to burden the exercise of religion, a "generally applicable and otherwise valid law" will be sustained regardless of its "incidental" effects on religious practices.

Employment Division, Department of Human Resources of Oregon v. Smith – 494 U.S. 872 (1990)

Two Native Americans who worked as counselors for a private drug rehabilitation organization, ingested peyote – a powerful hallucinogen – as part of their religious ceremonies as members of the Native American Church. As a result of this conduct, the rehabilitation organization fired the counselors. The counselors filed a claim for unemployment compensation. The government denied them benefits because the reason for their dismissal was considered work-related "misconduct". The counselors lost their battle in state court. But the U.S. Supreme Court vacated the Oregon Supreme Court's judgment against the disgruntled employees, and returned the case to the Oregon courts to determine whether or not sacramental use of illegal drugs violated Oregon's state drug laws (485 U.S. 660 (1988)). On remand, the Oregon Supreme Court concluded that while Oregon drug law prohibited the consumption of illegal drugs for sacramental religious uses, this prohibition violated the free exercise clause. The case returned to the U.S. Supreme Court in this new posture.

Berater
einnehmen – Peyote
Arbeitslosigkeit
Fehlerverhalten
außer Kraft setzen
verärgert

Issue

Does the state law violate the Free Exercise Clause of the First Amendment?

Holding and Reasoning

Antonin Scalia (1936 –)
Ass. Justice: 1986 –
Party: Republican
Appointed by: R. Reagan

No. Justice Scalia, writing for the majority, observed that the Court has never held that an individual's religious beliefs excuse him from compliance with an otherwise valid law prohibiting conduct that government is free to regulate. Allowing exceptions to every state law or regulation affecting religion "would open the prospect of constitutionally required exemptions from civic obligations of almost every conceivable kind". Scalia cited as examples compulsory military service, payment of taxes, vaccination requirements, and child-neglect laws.

Befolgung

Aussicht

zivile Pflichten

vorstellbar

Impfung – Vernachlässigung von Kindern

II. Past Uses of the Traditional Test

Whatever the status of the strict scrutiny test after Smith, there is a long history of the Court using a **compelling state interest** test to invalidate or uphold the application of neutral statutes or policies that affect religion. Principal among them was Wisconsin v. Yoder.

für ungültig erklären – wahren – Anwendung

State of Wisconsin v. Yoder – 406 U.S. 205 (1972)

Jonas Yoder and Wallace Miller, both members of the Old Order Amish religion, and Adin Yutzy, a member of

Amish, member of a conservative Christian group in North America, primarily members of the Old Order Amish Mennonite Church.
The Amish are best known for their severely plain clothing and their nonconformed way of life. This cultural nonconformity is thought by the Amish to be obedience to biblical strictures. Children attend public elementary schools and are not sent to high schools. This practice has caused the Amish some difficulty because of compulsory school attendance laws, and some Amish parents have gone to jail rather than allow their children to go to high school.

the Conservative Amish Mennonite Church, were prosecuted under a Wisconsin law that required all children to attend public schools until age 16. The three parents refused to send their children to such schools after the eighth grade, arguing that high school attendance was contrary to their religious beliefs.

strafrechtlich verfolgen

argumentieren
gegensätzlich

Issue

Did Wisconsin's requirement that all parents send their children to school at least until age 16 violate the First Amendment by criminalizing the conduct of parents who refused to send their children to school for religious reasons?

Erfordernis

kriminalisieren

Holding and Reasoning

Yes. In a 6-to-1 decision, the Court held that individual's interests in the free exercise of religion under the First Amendment outweighed the State's interests in compelling school attendance beyond the eighth grade. The Court found that the values and programs of secondary school were "in sharp conflict with the fundamental mode of life mandated by the Amish religion", and that an additional one or two years of high school would not produce the benefits of public education cited by Wisconsin to justify the law.

überwiegen

The Court has also held that church-affiliated schools are not subject to federal unemployment compensation laws and has construed federal labor laws narrowly, making them inapplicable to protect unionization activities of lay faculty at religious schools on the ground that government intervention would present "serious constitutional questions".

auslegen
unanwendbar – gewerkschaftliche Organisation

Diagram 18

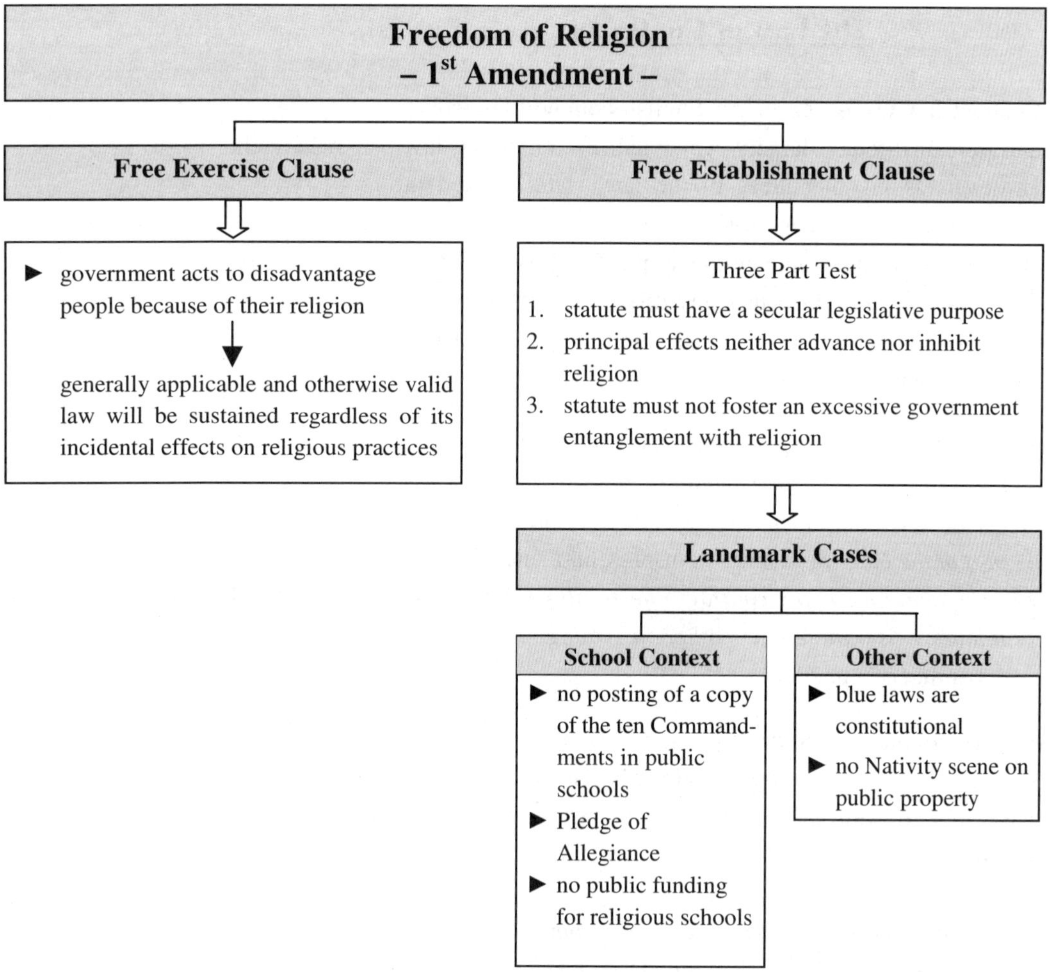

Further reading

Scott/Powell/Leon, Contract Law and Theory, 2nd ed., 1993; *Murray,* Contracts: Cases and Materials, 5th ed., 2000; *Macaulay e.a.,* Contracts: Law in Action, 1995; *Vernon,* Contracts: Theory and Practice, 2nd ed., 1991; *Corbin,* Contracts, 1993; *Williston,* A Treatise on the Law of Contracts, 4th ed., 1990; *Farnsworth,* Contracts, 1990; *Farnsworth,* United States Contract Law, 1991; *Craswell/ Schwartz,* Foundations on Contract Law, 1994; *Gilmore,* The Death of Contract, 1974; *Kronman/Posner,* The Economics of Contract Law.

Chapter Three

The Law of Contracts

Contract law originated in the English common law courts and remains today largely governed by common law. However, as in other areas of the law, state and federal statutes play an increasing role. — beherrscht

But despite this development the term contract is not a clear one. It has been defined in many different ways. Compare the following definitions to get an impression how difficult it is to say what the law of contracts is:

- *"A contract is an agreement enforceable at law, made between two or more persons, by which rights are acquired by one or more to acts or forbearances on the part of the other or others."* (Anson, Contracts, p. 11) — durchsetzbar; erwerben
- *"The act alone is the contract, the resulting contractual relation is quite a different thing."* (Holland, Jurisprudence, p. 251) — vertraglich

A very common definition is that a contract is a promise enforceable at law directly or indirectly. However, the best basis to start with is the defenition of the American Law Institute:

> *"A contract is a promise or a set of promises for the breach of which the law gives a remedy or the performance of which the law in some way recognizes as a duty."* (Contracts Restatement, § 1) — Bruch; Ausführung; Pflicht

In this chapter the focus is on the common law governing the law of contracts. The following issues will be discussed:

- **main characteristics of a contract** (part 1): how can we classify contracts? What are the necessary elements of a contract?
- **mutual assent** (part 2): How to make a valid offer and a valid acceptance? What is the right time to accept? What is the mail box rule? — gegenseitig

- **consideration** (part 3): What does the concept of consideration mean? Why is it necessary? What is the bargain, what is the detriment element?
- **formal requirements** (part 4): Must a contract be in writing? What is the parol evidence rule?
- **defenses to the contract's formation** (part 5): What happens if there are any defenses to the contract? Can a child enter into a valid contract? What is misrepresentation?
- **interpretation** (part 6): How can a contract be interpreted? Does the court decide on ambiguous terms?
- **performance and breach** (part 7): What is partial performance? How can a party breach its contractual obligation?
- **remedies** (part 8): What kind of remedies are there? How are damages measured? What is specific performance? What is laches?

The discussion will be very detailed if it is necessary to explain certain ideas and concepts that are unknown to the German lawyer or law student. However, things will be discussed briefly if they are only necessary for reasons of completeness.

Part 1: Introduction

A contract is a **<u>promise</u> or set of promises**, for breach of which the law gives a <u>remedy</u>, or the <u>performance</u> of which the law in some way recognizes as a duty.

Versprechen, Zusage
Rechtsbehelf – Erfüllung

<u>A. Types of Contracts</u>

<u>I. Express and Implied Contracts</u>

Contracts are described as express, implied, or quasi:
<u>Express contracts</u> are formed by language, oral or written.
<u>Implied contracts</u> are formed by manifestation or assent other than oral or written language, i.e., by conduct.

Ausdrücklicher Vertrag
Stillschweigender Vertrag

Upton-on-Severn Rural District v. Powell, 1 All E.R. 220 (C.A. 1942)

The defendant's barn was on fire and he called the local Upton police chief and asked him to send "the fire brigade". The Upton fire brigade showed up and began to put out the fire. While the fire was still burning, a neighboring fire chief came by and informed all that the farm was really in his district, and so the Upton fire brigade was not under obligation to put it out for free. When the defendant refused to pay for the service, they sued.

Stall

Verpflichtung

Issue

Was there a contract between the fire brigade and the farmer by implied promise of the farmer to pay if payment was required?

Holding and Reasoning

Yes. Parties create a contract by implied promise when one renders service that requires payment, even though the other may not be aware that the service requires payment. The court reasoned that the fact that neither intended to enter into a contract was irrelevant. The contract was created because the service was performed and therefore there was an implied promise to pay.

leisten – erfordern
bewusst

erfüllen

Quasi-contracts are not contracts at all. They are constructed by courts to avoid unjust enrichment by permitting the plaintiff to bring an action in restitution to recover the amount of the benefit conferred upon the defendant.

vertragsähnliches Verhältnis – auslegen – ungerechtfertigte Bereicherung – Kläger

II. Bilateral and Unilateral Contracts

One can distinguish between bilateral and unilateral contracts: The traditional **bilateral contract** was one consisting of the exchange of mutual promises, i.e. a promise for a promise in which each party is both a promisor and a promisee.

gegenseitiges Versprechen
Versprechensgeber – Versprechensempfänger

The traditional **unilateral contract** was one in which the offer requested performance rather than a promise. Here, the offeror-promisor would promise to pay upon the completion of the act by the promisee. Once the promise was completed, a contract was formed. In such contracts, there is one promisor and one promisee.

Erfüllung erfordern
Vollendung

III. Validity of Contracts

Furthermore, one can classify contracts as to validity:

A **void contract** is one that is totally without legal effect from the beginning (e.g. an agreement to commit a crime).

ungültig
begehen

A **voidable contract** is one that one or both parties may elect to avoid or to ratify (e.g., contracts of infants or mentally ill parties).

anfechtbar
ratifizieren – Kinder

An **unenforceable contract** is an agreement otherwise valid, but that may not be enforceable due to various defenses extraneous to contract formation, such as the Statute of Limitations or Statute of Fraud.

nicht erzwingbar/klagbar
aufgrund – Einrede/Einwendung – außerhalb
Verjährung – Formerfordernis

Diagram 19

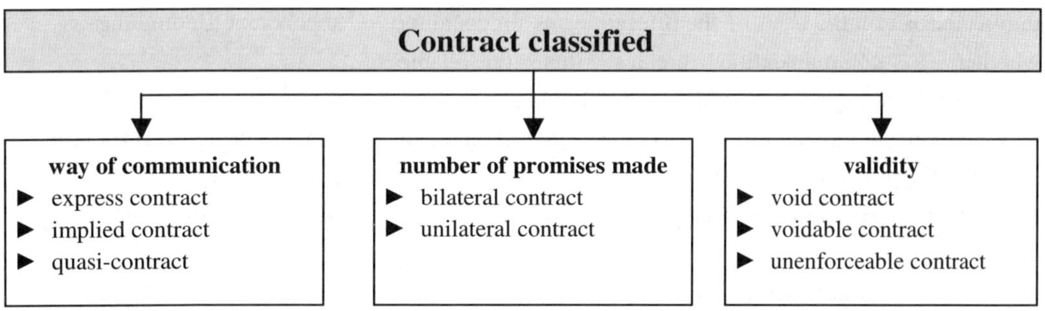

B. Elements Necessary for a Contract

There are mainly two elements that are necessary to form a contract.

First, mutual assent is needed consisting of **offer** and **acceptance** (see infra Part 2). Secondly, a contract requires **consideration** or one of its substitutes (see infra Part 3).

gegenseitige Zustimmung – Angebot – Annahme

Part 2: Mutual Assent

Mutual assent is said to be agreeing to the "same bargain at the same time" – "a meeting of the minds". The process by which parties reach the meeting of the minds generally is some form of negotiating, during which, at some point, **one party makes a proposal (an offer) and the other agrees to it (an acceptance)**. An actual subjective meeting of the minds is not necessary. Rather, courts use an objective measure, by which each party is bound to the apparent intention that he manifested to the other.

verhandeln
Vorschlag – Angebot
Annahme
offensichtlich
Wille

A. The Offer

An offer is a manifestation of willingness to enter into a bargain so made as to justify another person in understanding that his assent to that bargain is invited and will conclude it.

Handel

An offer creates a power of acceptance in the offeree and a corresponding liability on the part of the offeror. For a communication to be an offer, it must create a reasonable expectation in the offeree that the offeror is willing to enter into a contract on the basis of the offered terms. In deciding whether a communication creates this reasonable expectation, there are three questions one should ask:

Angebotsempfänger
Anbieter
angebotene Bedingung

- Was there an **expression** of a promise, undertaking, or commitment to enter into contract?
- Were there **certainty and definiteness** in the essential terms?
- Was there **communication** of the above to offeree?

Versprechen – Verpflichtung
Engagement
Sicherheit – Bestimmtheit

I. Promise, Undertaking or Commitment

The problem here is to distinguish between statements of future intent or preliminary negotiations on the one hand and statement of promise, undertaking, or commitment on the other. The criteria used to make this distinction are the following.

vorläufig

1. Language

The language used may show that an offer was or was not intended. **Technical language such as "I offer" or "I promise" is useful, but not necessary.** Certain language is generally construed as contemplating an invitation or preliminary negotiations.

auslegen

2. Surrounding Circumstances

The surrounding circumstances will be considered by courts in determining whether an offer exists. For example, where the **statement is made in jest, anger**, or by way of bragging, and the statement is reasonably understood in this context, it will have **no legal effect**. However, where the statement is subjectively intended to be in jest but reasonably understood by the hearer to have been made seriously, a contract results because of the **objective test**.

anschauen, abwägen

Spaß – Zorn

prahlen, angeben

3. Advertisement

Advertisements, catalogs, circular letters, and the like containing price quotations are usually construed as mere **invitations for offers**. They are announcements of prices at which the seller is willing to receive offers. In certain situations, courts have treated advertisements as offers where the language of the advertisement can be construed as containing a promise, where the terms are certain and definite, and where the offeree is clearly identified.

Werbung – Rundschreiben

auslegen

Rhen Marshall, Inc. v. Purolator Filter Div., 211 Neb. 306, 318 N.W.2d 284 (1982).

Purolator sent Rhen Marshall an advertising circular containing a list of premiums dealers could receive if they ordered a certain number of its products. Under "Deal 5A", an order for 100,000 pounds of Purolator products earned the dealer a Buick Electra and 100 Kodak instant cameras. The circular did not mention billing or discount terms. Rhen Marshall responded with a purchase order for the correct amount of goods for "Deal 5A," which it specified. It also requested a 5 percent truckload discount and 30-60-90-day billing--the terms of its previous contracts with Purolator. Purolator rejected the order. Rhen Marshall sued for damages, claiming the circular was an offer which its order accepted. The trial court dismissed the complaint.

Zahlungs- und Rabattbedingungen; vorgehend; abweisen; klagen; zurückweisen

Issue

Had Purolator made an offer which Rhen Marshall could accept?

Holding and Reasoning

No. The advertisement of goods for sale at a certain price is not an offer. An advertisement invites a proposal of a bargain.

The proposal is not an offer to be turned into an agreement by acceptance, even when directed to definite persons. Advertising circulars go no further than what occurs when someone asks what another will give or take for certain goods. The circulars ask for offers which the advertiser has a right to accept or to reject.

Übereinkunft; richten an

II. Definiteness and Certainty

An offer must be **definite and certain in its terms**. The basic inquiry is whether enough of the essential terms have been provided so that a contract including them would be capable of being enforced. The principle is that the parties make their own contract; the courts do not make it for them. What is essential for the requisite certainty is an offer. It will, of course, depend upon the kind of contract contemplated. The "essential" elements list includes:

- **identity** of offeree and subject matter
- **price** to be paid
- **time** of payment, delivery or performance
- **quantity** involved
- **nature of work** to be performed

Frage; durchsetzbar; notwendig; Lieferung

Anderson v. Backlund, 159 Minn. 423, 199 NW 90 (1924)

The plaintiff was having difficulty "making ends meet" because the crop was poor on the farm land he leased from the defendant. The plaintiff alleges that the defendant agreed to provide enough water for 100 additional head of cattle, if he would put them to pasture on his land. The water supply failed, however, and so the then 174 head of cattle lost value due to starvation, and the plaintiff was damaged in the sum of $2,500. Both parties assume the risk of fulfilling exactly the terms of the contract, however absurd or improbable, as long as it remains possible to fulfill that contract.

Ziel erreichen
Ernte
Vieh – weiden
Hungern
annehmen

Issue

Was there a contract between the plaintiff and the defendant?

Holding and Reasoning

No. Contracts must be in certain terms and not so indefinite and illusory as to make it impossible to say just what is promised. The language between the plaintiff and the defendant was taken as advice and not a contract, and so the court concluded there was no contract.

unbestimmt

To be considered an offer, a statement must sufficiently identify the offeree or a class to which he belongs to justify the inference that the offeror intended to create a power of acceptance.

The subject matter of the deal must be certain, since a court can enforce a promise only if it can tell with reasonably accuracy what the promise is. It will generally be enforceable even if it does not spell out every material term, as long as it contains some objective standard to supply the missing terms.

Rückschluss
Gegenstand
Exaktheit

B. Acceptance

An acceptance of an offer is "a **manifestation of assent** to the terms thereof made by the offeree in a manner invited or required by the offer."

Ausdruck – Zustimmung

I. Means of Acceptance

The common law makes a distinction between "bilateral" contracts (where the offeror seeks acceptance through a promise of performance) and "unilateral" contracts (where the offeror seeks acceptance through actual performance). The offeror, as the master of the offer, may prescribe the method by which the offer will be accepted.

zweiseitig
Erfüllung – einseitig

1. Acceptance by Mail – The Mailbox Rule

The common law follows the **"mailbox rule"**, whereby the acceptance becomes effective upon mailing the acceptance. **Since the acceptance is effective when mailed, the contract is concluded at that time.** Thus the offeror will only learn of the acceptance and existence of the contract when he actually receives it. If an offeree mails an acceptance, but later reconsiders and communicates a rejection, the rejection is not valid even if it arrives before the acceptance. This rule prevents an offeree from accepting an offer using, for example, slow mail service, while knowing that if market prices suddenly change or a better offer is submitted by someone else, he can quickly dispatch an overtaking rejection. But if a rejection is sent first and the offeree after reflection sends an overtaking acceptance, the acceptance will be effective if it arrives before the rejection.

„Briefkasten-Regel"
zulässig, gültig
abhalten
abfertigen, befördern
überholen

Cushing v. Thomson, 386 A.2d 805 (1978)

The plaintiff is a representative of an anti-nuclear group that wanted to hold a dance at the local National Guard hall represented by the defendant. The defendant filled out an application, and the defendant mailed an offer to be accepted within 5 days. The plaintiff signed the offer, and put it in the mail drop box, which was customarily mailed every day. That night, the defendant called the plaintiff and told him that the offer was revoked. The plaintiff claimed that the offer could not be revoked because it was already accepted based on his mailing. Trial court held for the plaintiff and granted specific performance.

Anmeldung, Antrag
zurückziehen
Leistung der Vertragsschuld

Issue
In the case of negotiations by mail, can an offeror revoke after the offeree has put his acceptance in the mail?

Holding and Reasoning
No. A contract negotiated through the mail becomes binding when the offeree posts his acceptance in the mail. The plaintiff introduced sworn affidavits that he put the letter of acceptance in the mail before the call by the defendant. The defendant did not argue. The use of mail for acceptance is sufficient when the offer was communicated by mail. The offeree can not control the mail delivery once the letter is delivered.

eidesstattliche Versicherung

genug

Notes
The policy is that to require actual notice would lead to an infinite exchange of notification between the parties. The plaintiff would notify acceptance, then the defendant would have to notify the plaintiff of receipt and assent to the acceptance, etc.
Revocations, however, are generally held to be effective only upon actual notice. Some states have statutes overruling this requirement. The person making the contract is always free to make the offer contingent upon actual notice of acceptance.

unbegrenzt

Erhalt – Zustimmung

aufheben
abhängig, bedingt

2. Acceptance by Silence

An offer may also be accepted by silence but special rules apply:

Cole-McIntyre-Norfleet Co. v. Holloway, 214 SW 817 (Tenn. 1919)

A traveling salesman representing Holloway (seller) solicited and received an order from Cole (buyer) for 50 barrels of meal, to be delivered before the 31st of July. If the barrels were not delivered by then, Holloway would charge Cole 5 cents/barrel/mo. for storage. The salesman continued to make weekly calls on Cole, never mentioning

Händler
erbitten
Fass

Lagerung

the previous order. Meanwhile, prices went up 50%. On May 26th, Cole asked for delivery, but Holloway refused claiming that they had never accepted the order, and so there was no contract.

Lieferung
behaupten

Issue

Did the sixty-day silence of the seller bar him from claiming that he had refused the order, thus resulting in no contract?

abhalten, hindern

Holding and Reasoning

No. When the nature of goods, or the market conditions surrounding those goods, requires prompt action on the part of the contracting parties, the silent stalling of one of the parties constitutes an action from which assent may be inferred.

hinhalten
ableiten, folgen

The salesman had weekly opportunities to inform the buyer, and the seller had daily opportunities to inform the buyer of the refusal of the order. The fact that there was no official refusal, coupled with conduct of "business-as-usual" by both parties was sufficient to provide assent. To hold otherwise would be to give the seller the reservation of power to hold the buyer to the contract, while allowing the seller to exit the contract if the price went down. This would assign all risk to the buyer.

Möglichkeit
Ablehnung
Verhalten
Vorbehalt

3. Acceptance by Performance

A third way of accepting an offer is when one of the parties start performing:

Underwood Typewriter Co. v. Century Realty Co. – 220 Mo. 522, 119 S.W. 400 (1909)

The plaintiff leased a building from the defendant. The lease stated that the plaintiff could not sublet without the written permission of the defendant. The plaintiff and the defendant also entered into a written agreement that the defendant promised to give written assent for the plaintiff

Erlaubnis

to sublet to an "acceptable tenant". The plaintiff, relying on defendant's promise, spent considerable effort and found a suitable tenant, who was willing to pay a higher rent than the plaintiff currently paid. But the defendant refused to allow the plaintiff to sublet. The plaintiff sued for the profits it would have made if it would have sublet. The defendant demurred. Trial court sustained the demurrer. Appellant court reversed and remanded for trial.

untervermieten – Mieter – vertrauen – Anstrengung

Gewinn

Einspruch erheben – Einspruch stattgeben – aufheben – zurückverwiesen

Issue

Is there a contract supported by plaintiff's reliance on defendant's promise?

Holding and Reasoning

Yes. Contracts may be formed by the offer of a promise for an act and the acceptance by performing the act.

The court reasoned that the performance by the promisee was sufficient consideration to support a contract, even though the promisor gained no benefit. This is the standard reliance principle.

verdienen

Vertrauen

II. Time for Acceptance

The power to accept an offer does not belong to the offeree forever. However, an offer may be **irrevocable**.

1. Means of Termination

There are mainly **three ways how an offer can be terminated**.

a) Lapse

The period of acceptance can be terminated by lapse, rejection, revocation, or the death of a party. Often the offer specifies the amount of time in which the offer may be accepted by the offeree. If the offeree does not accept within that time, the offer has lapsed, and the offeree can no longer exercise a power to accept and close the deal. If no period is specified in the offer, it lapses after a reasonable time or

Verfall, Ablauf

ausüben

angemessen

until the offeror revokes the offer. What is a reasonable time depends on the circumstances.
For example, unless specified otherwise, an offer made in a face-to-face conversation is usually deemed to continue only to the close of the conversation, and cannot be accepted thereafter. — angesehen, erachtet

b) Rejection

The power to accept an offer also ends when the offeree rejects the offer. After rejecting the offer, the offeree cannot change his mind and accept. An offeree's **counter-offer terminates his power of acceptance** just as if he had rejected the offer, unless the original offer is irrevocable. An offeree can avoid this result by using language which does not reject the offer. — rejects: zurückweisen, ablehnen; counter-offer: Gegenangebot

c) Revocation

Before the offeree accepts or rejects the offer, the offeror can terminate the offeree's power of acceptance by revoking the offer. A revocation sent by the offeror is effective upon receipt by the offeree. Thus the issue of when the acceptance becomes effective may be an important question in determining if the offeror still has the power to revoke the offer or if it has already been accepted. — revoking: zurücknehmen; receipt: Erhalt

Dickinson v. Dodds – Ct. App. Chancery Div., 2 Ch. Div. 463 (1876)

On Wednesday, the defendant wrote a letter to the plaintiff stating that he was offering his property for sale to the plaintiff a certain sum, and that the offer was good until Friday at 9am. The defendant then offered to sell to another on Thursday. The plaintiff brought a letter of acceptance to the defendant on Friday morning at 7am. The defendant refused the letter, stating that he was too late, and the property was already sold. The plaintiff sued for specific performance. — property: Eigentum; good: gültig; specific performance: Leistung der Vertragsschuld

Issue

Whether an offer that states that it is good for a period of time (a firm offer) can be revoked by the offeror at any time before the acceptance by the offeree?

Holding and Reasoning

A statement to make an offer valid for a length of time does not bind the offeror.

The court reasoned that the defendant was free at any time to rescind the offer, because it had not been accepted by the plaintiff, and a contract would not become binding until there was "agreement" between both parties.

aufheben

Notes

This is a classical contract theory court. The modern view under the reliance doctrine would be that the risk was redistributed by the promise by the defendant that the offer was valid until Friday morning, and the resultant reliance by the plaintiff on that promise.

umverteilen

2. Irrevocability

For the protection of the offeree, there are some situations in which an offer is **irrevocable** for a period of time. An offer is irrevocable if the offeree gives the offeror "consideration" for a promise not to revoke the offer for a period of time. Giving consideration means that the **offeree pays or otherwise gives value to the offeror** to keep the offer "open" for some period of time. An offeree in this position is said to have an "option contract," and may consider the offer for the period of time agreed upon without fear of revocation.

unwiderrufbar

(see infra, part 3)

a) Part Performance

Normally an offer also becomes irrevocable once the offeree renders **part performance**. Where the offeror wants acceptance by performance, an option contract is created when the offeree begins the invited performance. The length

leisten – Teilerfüllung

of this option contract is a "reasonable time." Since an offer for a unilateral contract has not been accepted until the offeree has fully performed, this rule protects the offeree from revocation after he has started to perform, but has not yet fully performed.

b) Offeree relies on the Offer

Under some circumstances, an offer can be irrevocable when the offeree relies on the offer, but has not yet begun performance. Thus, an offer which the offeror should reasonably expect to induce action or forbearance of a substantial character on the part of the offeree before acceptance and which does induce such action or forbearance is binding as an option contract to the extent necessary to avoid injustice.

vertrauen

verursachen – unterlassen

Diagram 20

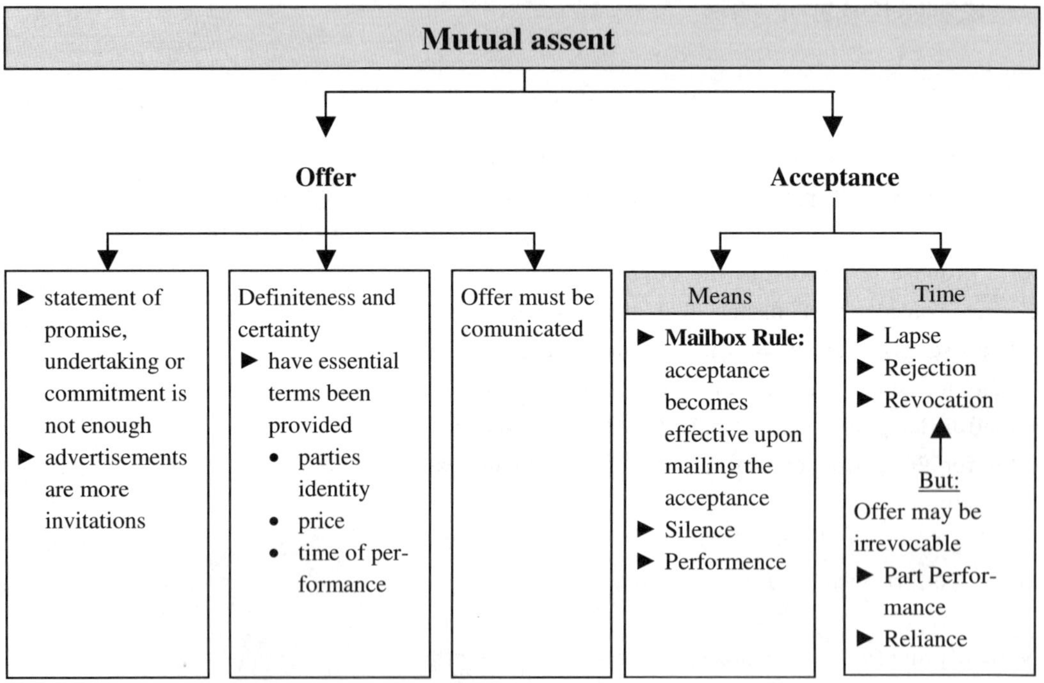

Part 3: Consideration

A. Introduction

The common law countries adhere to the doctrine of consideration. In 1768 the House of Lords concluded:

> *"All contracts are, by the laws of England, distinghuished into agreements by specialty [i.e. agreements under seal] and agreements by parol; nor is there any such third class as some of the counsel have endeavored to maintain, as contracts in writing. If they be merely written and not specialties, they are parol, and **a consideration must be proved**." (Rann v. Hughes, 7 T.R. 350n, 101 Eng.Rep. 1014n)*

mündlich

sich bemühen

Thus, as a general rule, a contract will not be enforceable unless it is supported by "consideration." A promise is supported by consideration if:

erzwingbar, durchsetzbar

- The promise is given as part of a "bargain"; that is, the promisor makes his promise in exchange for the promisee's giving of value.
- The promisee gives up something of value, or circumscribes his liberty in some way (i.e., he suffers a "legal detriment").

Handel

einschränken

Nachteil, Schaden

The requirement of consideration renders unenforceable two main types of transactions:

- **Promises to make gifts** (which do not satisfy the "bargain" element); and
- **Business situations** in which one party has not really promised to do something or given anything up, even though he may appear to have done so (the "detriment" element is missing here).

B. The Bargain Element

A promise to make a gift is generally unenforceable, because it lacks the "bargain" element of consideration.

Siegel v. Spear & Co. – 138 NE 414 (NY 1923)

The plaintiff bought furniture from the defendant, making monthly payments. Upon deciding to leave the city for the summer, the plaintiff asked the defendant to store plaintiff's furniture at defendant's warehouse. The defendant stated that they would store the furniture for free, and promised to obtain insurance for the furniture so that the plaintiff didn't have to do so. Relying on this promise, the plaintiff sent the furniture over. However, the defendant did not obtain the promised insurance, and it was subsequently destroyed in a fire.

Möbel
Versicherung
vertrauen
anschließend

Issue

Whether the defendant is liable for the value of the furniture when he offered to store it for free (no consideration), and when he accepted possession of it?

Holding and Reasoning

"If a person makes a gratuitous promise, and then enters upon the performance of it, he is held to a full execution of all he has undertaken."

The confidence placed in the promisor and his undertaking to complete the trust create a sufficient consideration to find a contract. Had there been no delivery of the furniture, there would have been no contract - only a gratuitous promise. However, once the furniture had been delivered in reliance on the promise of insurance, a consideration was created.

kostenlos
Ausführung
Vertrauen
Lieferung

I. Existence of Condition

Even if the person promising to make a gift requires the promisee to meet certain **conditions** in order to receive the gift, there will still be **no consideration** (and the promise will thus be unenforceable) if the meeting of the conditions is not really "bargained for" by the promisor.

erfordern
Bedingung

Kirksey v. Kirksey – 8 Ala. 131 (1845)

The plaintiff is the widow of the defendant's brother. When the defendant heard of his brother's death, he sent a letter to the plaintiff advising her to sell whatever interest she had in the land she was presently on, and to move her family to his farm. He promised that "[i]f you will come down and see me, I will let you have a place to raise your family, and I have more open land than I can tend...." The plaintiff abandoned her land, and moved down to the defendant's land. After 2 years of cultivating his land, he eventually told her to leave.

Witwe
Recht
großziehen
pflegen
verlassen

Issue

Is there sufficient consideration to find a binding contract based on the plaintiff's moving and giving up what she had?

Holding and Reasoning

No. A promise which is a mere gratuity does not create a binding contract. The writer of the opinion reasoned that there was sufficient consideration because she had moved, but they reversed anyway.

But if the promisor imposes a condition, and the occurrence of this condition is of benefit to him, then the bargain element probably will be present.

Hamer v. Sidway, - NY Ct. App., 27 N.E. 256 (1891)

The plaintiff is the nephew of a man who promised him $5,000 on his 21st birthday if he would abstain from smoking, drinking, or playing cards, etc. The plaintiff did abstain and let his uncle know. The uncle then responded with a letter stating that the money would continue to collect interest until the plaintiff was able to take care of it. The uncle then died, and the executor refused to give the money to the plaintiff, claiming that there was no consideration, and that the plaintiff did not act to his detriment, because abstinence actually was to his benefit.

sich enthalten
Zinsen
Testamentsvollstrecker
Nachteil

Issue

Is there a binding contract based on consideration, even though the actions were to the benefit of the plaintiff even without the promise?

Holding and Reasoning

Yes. A contracting party does not need to perform an act or forbearance that is of any value to anyone in order for there to be sufficient consideration to support contract formation. It is sufficient that the party perform the act or forbearance requested.

Unterlassen

The court reasoned that the plaintiff had a legal right to use tobacco, or to drink, and that by abandoning that right in reliance on his uncle's promise, he was entitled to the $5,000.

verlassen
Vertrauen

But the fact that one who promises to make a gift expects to derive **altruistic pleasure, or love** and affection, from making the gift is **not sufficient to constitute a "bargain."**

erhalten – selbstlos – Zunei-gung

It is only the promise to make a gift, not the actual making of a gift, that is unenforceable for lack of consideration. Once the promisor makes the gift, he cannot rescind it for lack of consideration.

aufheben

II. Sham and Nominal Consideration

Even though a deal looks on its face as if it is supported by consideration, the court may conclude that the purported consideration is **sham or nominal**, and is thus not consideration at all.

vorgetäuscht

1. Nominal Amount

Thus where the "consideration" that has been paid is **so small as to be nominal**, the court may conclude as a factual matter that there is **no real "bargain"** present at all. If so, the promise will not be enforced, due to lack of consideration.

folgen

But if the consideration is big enough to suggest that there was a bargain, the fact that it is "inadequate" is irrelevant.	annehmen unangemessen

2. Payment Not in Fact Made

If a non-trivial payment is recited, but the payment was not in fact made, most courts will take this as evidence that no bargain was present. Always, the question is whether there was in fact a bargain, and payment or non-payment is merely non-dispositive evidence of whether there was a bargain.	vortragen Beweis nicht entscheidend – Beweis

III. "Past Consideration"

If the promise is made in return for **detriment previously suffered** by the promisee, there is no bargain, and thus no consideration. Thus promises to pay a pre-existing debt, and promises to pay for services already received, usually lack the "bargain" element.	bereits bestehend Dienstleistung – erhalten

Lingenfelder v. The Wainwright Brewing Co., 103 Mo. 578, 15 SW 844 (1891)

The plaintiff was hired by the defendant as an architect to design and build a brewery for 5% commission on the cost of the buildings. After the plaintiff started performance, the defendant awarded a contract for a refrigerator, against the plaintiff's wishes, to a competitor. The plaintiff stopped performance in protest, and said he would not finish. The defendant, out of haste to have the brewery finished, offered the plaintiff an additional 5% commission on the refrigerator so that he would continue work. At the conclusion, the defendant did not want to pay the extra 5% because he claimed that the promise was without consideration since the plaintiff was already under contract to perform. The plaintiff sued claiming that a new contract was formed by the new offer.	Brauerei Wettbewerb in Eile

Issue

Whether the promise by the defendant to pay more money to convince the plaintiff not to breach was a binding new offer? — überzeugen

Holding and Reasoning

No. "[A] promise to pay a man for doing that which he is already under contract to do is without consideration."
The court reasoned that the defendant received no "benefit" from the new promise, and that the plaintiff was not required to do anything more than he was already obligated to do. The court saw it as outright extortion, done in bad faith, and refuted the plaintiff's argument that he would be "detrimented" if a competitor were allowed to install the refrigerator. They further refuted the idea that since the plaintiff defaulted, the defendant was entitled to sue for breach, and having not elected to sue, he was estopped from claiming that his promise was without consideration. It would be assumed that if he forewent the opportunity to sue, that he recognized that he was gaining value from the additional promise.

verpflichtet – äußerst – Wucher
widerlegen
säumig sein – berechtigt sein
ausgeschlossen
nutzen

C. The "Detriment" Element

For consideration to be present, the promisee must suffer a "detriment." That is, **he must do something he does not have to do, or refrain from doing something that he has a right to do**.

Verlust

I. Pre–Existing Duty and Promises

A party who does or promises to do only what the party is legally obligated to do is not suffering a legal detriment because the party is not surrendering a legal right. The problem arises in three types of fact patterns. First, the rule applies even if the duty is imposed by law rather than by contract. Second, where the parties to a contract modify an existing agreement and one party does not suffer new detriment, usually the modification is not enforced, but there

abgeben
gelten
modifizieren
durchsetzbar

are cases that, on a wide variety of theories, have enforced such a modification. For example, The Restatement (Second) upholds such a modification if it "is fair and equitable in view of circumstances not anticipated when the contract is made." Third, where an outsider promises to compensate a party bound by a contract to perform a pre-existing duty under a contract, there are two views.

auf Billigkeitsrecht beruhend – vorhersehen

- The promise is not enforceable;
- The promise is enforceable because there is less likelihood of coercion in the three party cases.

Zwang

II. Illusory and Implied Promises

1. Illusory Promises

An "illusory" promise is not supported by consideration, and is therefore not enforceable. An illusory promise is a statement which appears to be promising something, but which in fact does not commit the promisor to do anything at all.

illusorisch

2. Implied Promises

Courts try to avoid striking down agreements for lack of consideration. One way they do this is by finding that the promisee has made an implied promise in return.

implizieren, beinhalten – Versprechen

Wood v. Lucy, Lady Duff-Gordon, 97 NY Supp. 566 (1917)

The defendant is a "creator of fashion" who gave the plaintiff the exclusive right, subject to her ultimate approval, to market her name as an endorsement. She was to receive half of the profits, and he was to obtain any necessary patents, copyrights, etc. to protect her interests. The defendant sold her name to others on the side, and the plaintiff sued for damages. The defendant claims that there were not the elements of a contract because the plaintiff had no obligation to sell anything of hers.

abhängig von
Zustimmung – Empfehlung

Rechte

behaupten

Issue

Is there consideration on the part of the plaintiff as found by the actions and relationship of the parties sufficient to find a contract, even though there was no explicit amount of sales of the defendant's name that he had to make?

Holding and Reasoning

Yes. Where there is not an explicit obligation in a written contract for the amount a person will perform, it may be implied that the person is obligated to perform using reasonable efforts [in good faith].

The court reasoned that the contract did not fail because of the mechanical wording. They implied a meaning based on the actions and the relationship of the parties. Viewing the contract as a whole, it was evident that both parties expected the plaintiff to make reasonable efforts to make profits.

guter Glaube

Bedeutung

offensichtlich

Diagram 21

Consideration

Bargain

- gifts lack the bargain elements, even if the gift is conditional
- sham or nominal amounts are not enough
- "past consideration" lacks the bargain element

Detrimement

- pre-existing duty
- illusory promises
- implied promises

Part 4: Formal Requirements

Once there is mutual assent supported by consideration, an enforceable contract exists. There is no requirement for any formal ceremony to make the agreement "official", no requirement for a seal, and, in some cases, no requirement that the contract even be in writing. If the contract is in writing it does not have to be in any particular form. However, some types of contracts are required to be in writing under the "Statute of Frauds."

Erfordernis

Siegel

Schriftformerfordernis

A. The Statute of Frauds

All of the states (except Louisiana) have adopted a close form of the English Statute of Frauds (1677), which requires that certain types of contracts must be in writing in order to be enforceable. The primary purpose of the Statute of Frauds is to ensure that certain contracts are not enforced unless there is sufficient proof that the contract exists. There are five categories of contracts which, in almost every state, fall within the Statute of Frauds and must therefore be in writing:

annehmen, sich zu Eigen machen
versichern

- **Executor**: A contract of an executor or administrator to answer for the duty of his decedent;
- **Suretyship**: A contract to answer for the debt or duty of another.
- **Marriage**: A contract made upon consideration of marriage.
- **Land contract**: A contract for the sale of an interest in land.
- **One year**: A contract that cannot be performed within one year from its making.
- **U.C.C.**: Additionally, under the U.C.C., contracts for the sale of goods must be in writing if they are for a price of $500 or more.

Verwalter
Erblasser
erfüllen

B. Categories of Contract

I. Suretyship

A promise to pay the debt or duty of another is within the Statute of Frauds, and is therefore unenforceable unless in writing.
If the promisor's chief purpose in making his promise of suretyship is to further his own interest, his promise does not fall within the Statute of Frauds. This is called the "main purpose" rule.

Hauptzweck
Bürgschaft

II. Marriage

A promise for which the consideration is marriage or a promise of marriage is within the Statute.

Heirat

But if an <u>oral</u> contract consists solely of mutual promises to marry (with no <u>ancillary</u> promises regarding <u>property</u> transfers), the contract is not within the Statute of Frauds, and is enforceable even though oral. That is, an ordinary oral engagement is an enforceable contract.	mündlich zusätzlich – Eigentum

III. Land Contracts

1. Generally

A promise to transfer or buy any <u>interest in land</u> is within the Statute. The Statute does not apply to the <u>conveyance</u> itself (which is governed by separate statutes everywhere) but rather to a **contract providing for the <u>subsequent</u> conveyance of land**.	Grundstücksrecht Übertragung nachfolgend

2. Interests in Land

The Statute applies to promises to transfer not only a <u>fee simple interest</u> in land, but to transfer most other kinds of interests in land (see infra, chapter 6, volume 2).	unbeschränktes Eigentumsrecht

a) Leases/Mortgages

For instance, a <u>lease</u> is generally an "interest in land," so that a promise to make a lease will generally be <u>unenforceable</u> if not in writing. But most states have statutes making oral leases enforceable if their <u>duration</u> is **one year or less**. A promise to give a <u>mortgage</u> on real property as <u>security</u> for a <u>loan</u> also usually comes within the Statute.	Pacht, Miete nicht durchsetzbar Dauer Hypothek Sicherheit – Darlehen

b) Contracts Incidentally Related to Land

But contracts that <u>relate</u> only incidentally to land are not within the Statute. Thus a contract to build a building is not within the Statute, nor is a promise to lend money with which the borrower will buy land.	beziehen auf
Usually, the fact that the <u>vendee</u> has paid the <u>vendor</u> the purchase price under the oral agreement is not by itself	Käufer – Verkäufer

sufficient to make the contract enforceable. Instead, the vendee can simply recover the purchase price in a non-contract action for restitution.

IV. One Year

1. General Rule

If a promise contained in a contract is **incapable of being fully performed within one year after** the making of the contract, the contract must be in writing. — unfähig

The one-year period is measured from the time of execution of the contract, not the time it will take the parties to perform. — Ausführung, Durchführung

2. Impossibility

The one-year provision applies only if **complete performance is impossible within one year** after the making of the contract. The fact that performance within one year is highly unlikely is not enough. — unwahrscheinlich

It will often be hard to tell whether a certain kind of possible termination is by performance or by discharge. The test is whether, if the termination in question occurs, the contract has fulfilled its principal purpose. If it has fulfilled this purpose, there has been performance; if it has not, there has not been performance.

3. Termination

Courts are split about whether the existence of a termination clause that permits termination in less than a year will remove a more-than-one-year contract from the one-year provision. — gespalten

V. Sale of Goods

U.C.C. § 2-201(1) says that — Uniform Commercial Code

> *"a contract for the sale of goods for the price of $500 or more is not enforceable...unless there is some writing sufficient to indicate that a contract for sale has been made...."*

This rule will be discussed in the next chapter.

C. "In Writing"

The meaning of being "in writing" can be explained by the following case:

Crabtree v. Elizabeth Arden Sales Corporation – 110 N.E.2d 551 (1953)

In September 1947, the plaintiff began negotiating with the defendant for the position of the latter's sales manager. Being unfamiliar with the cosmetics business and giving up a well-paying, secure job, the plaintiff insisted upon an agreement for a definite term. He asked for three years at $ 25.000 per year. But the defendant offered two years, with $ 20.000 per year the first six months, $ 25.000 per year the second six months, and $ 30.000 per year the second year. This was written down by defendant's personal secretary with the notation "2 years to make good". A few days later, the plaintiff telephoned Mr. Johns, defendant's executive vice president, his acceptance. The plaintiff received a "welcome" wire from Miss Arden. When he reported for work, a "payroll change" card was made up and initialed by Mr. Johns showing the above pay arrangement with a salary increase noted "as per contractual agreement". The plaintiff received his first pay raise as scheduled, but not his second one. The defendant allegedly refused to approve the second increase, denying plaintiff had been hired for any specific period.

verhandeln
nicht gewohnt
Annahme
Gehaltsliste
Gehaltszuwachs
ablehnen, verweigern

Issue

Is there satisfactory evidence to piece together from separate documents a written contract within the Statute of Frauds, thus enforceable?

Beweis

Holding and Reasoning

Yes. First, as it is alleged that the contract is for a period of two years, there must be written evidence of its terms to be enforceable as the two-year performance places it within

behaupten

the Statute of Frauds. The payroll cards, one initialed by defendant's executive vice-president and the other by its comptroller, unquestionably constituted a memorandum under the statute. It is enough that they were signed with the intent to authenticate the information contained therein and that such information does evidence the terms of the contract. The cards had all essential terms except for duration. But as the memorandum can be pieced together from more than one document, all that is required between the papers is a connection established simply by reference to the same subject matter or transaction. Parol evidence is permissible in order to establish the connection. As the note prepared by defendant's personal secretary shows it was made in Miss Arden's presence as well as that of Johns and of plaintiff, the dangers of parol evidence are at a minimum. All of the terms must be set out in writing and cannot be shown by parol. That memo, the paper signed by Johns, and the paper signed by the comptroller all refer on their face to the plaintiff transaction. The comptroller's paper shows that it was prepared for the purpose of a "salary increase per contractual arrangements with Miss Arden". That is a reference to more comprehensive evidence and parol evidence can so explain. "2 years to make good" probably had no other purpose than to denote the duration of the arrangement and parol evidence may explain its meaning.

darstellen
Absicht
Bestandteile, Bedingung
erforderlich
mündlich
zulässig
Verweis, Hinweis
bedeuten
Dauer

Diagram 22

Statute of Frauds

adopted by all 50 states but Louisiana

General rule: contracts need not be in writing unless they fall in one of the following six categories

Excecuter	**Suretyship**	**Marrige**	**Land Contract**	**One Year Provision**	**Sale of Goods**
contract of an executer to answer for the duty of his decedent	contract to answer for the debt of another	contract made upon consideration of a marrige	► transfer or purchase of any interest in land • interest: bases, mortgages ► rule does not apply to contracts to build a house	► contract cannot be fullfilled wihtin one year after the making of the contract	U.C.C. § 2-201(1) see: Sales, Chapter 4, volume 2

D. The Parol Evidence Rule

I. Introduction and Purpose

A frequent problem occurs when a contract has been reduced to writing, but **one of the parties claims that their actual agreement included a term which is not in the writing**. The "parol evidence rule" determines whether the party may show evidence of a term that was allegedly agreed to before or at the time the writing was made, but was not included in the writing. The parol evidence rule generally **prohibits the introduction of extrinsic evidence that contradicts terms of a written contract**. The purpose of the parol evidence rule is to promote certainty by preventing written agreements from being contradicted by less reliable accounts of the agreement and by encouraging parties to make their written agreements complete. Although "parol" literally means "oral," the parol evidence rule acts to exclude not only oral evidence, but all forms of evidence extrinsic to the written agreement.

niedergelegt
angeblich
verbieten – nicht Bestandteil einer Urkunde – widersprechen
fördern
wörtlich
Beweis

II. The Rule

The parol evidence rule provides that, if a written contract is intended to be the final expression of the entire agreement and to include all of the terms and details of the agreement, no oral or "parol" evidence of terms may be supplied. If the contract is not intended to include all the details of the agreement, **evidence of terms that contradict the written contract will not be allowed**, but the party may show evidence of additional terms that do not contradict the writing. If the writing is not intended to constitute the full agreement, then parol evidence can be used to supplement or even contradict the terms of the writing. In the past the decision of the question of whether a written contract embodies the complete agreement of the parties was made by **looking solely at the document and determining if the terms sought to be added by parol evidence would naturally and normally have been left out of the writing**. But under the more modern approach a judge balances the actual intentions of the parties against the document itself.
The parol evidence rule applies only to extrinsic agreements that were made prior to or contemporaneous with the written agreement. It does not bar evidence that the contract was orally modified after the writing.

beabsichtigt
darstellen
ergänzen
verkörpern
Ansatz
tatsächlich
gleichzeitig

Thompson v. Libby – Minn. Sup. Ct., 34 Minn. 374, 26 N.W. 1 (1885)

Plaintiff and defendant entered into a contract for the sale of logs. The contract contained all necessary terms. The defendant later refused to pay for the logs. The plaintiff brought a suit for the contract price and the defendant defended on the basis of a parol contemporary warranty which was allegedly breached by the plaintiff. At trial, the court allowed the introduction of evidence concerning the warranty of quality orally given at the time of sale. It found for the defendant on this basis.

Holz, Baumstamm
Vertragspreis
Zusicherung
im Prozess

Issue
May parol evidence be admitted to prove the existence of a contemporary parol warranty?

Holding and Reasoning

No. In the case of a sale of personal property a warranty of quality is considered a part of the contract and not a collateral contract. The contract contains all necessary terms and is complete on its face. The parol evidence rule provides that contemporaneous parol evidence may not be admitted to contradict or vary the terms of a written contract which is complete on its face. Since a warranty is considered a contract term, it must be included in the contract. Parol evidence cannot be admitted to show that the contract is not a complete statement of the parties' agreement. The judge must determine whether the contract, based on its terms, represents the complete embodiment of the agreement. Since the contract is complete on its face, the trial court was incorrect in allowing the parol evidence of the warranty to be admitted.

Eigentum

begleitend, Neben-

zulassen

erachten

III. Rule Does Not Apply

There are mainly four areas in which the rule does not apply.

1. Fraud and Duress

Even if a writing is a total integration, a party may always introduce evidence of earlier oral agreements to show illegality, fraud, duress, mistake, lack of consideration, or any other fact that would make the contract void or voidable. In other words, the parol evidence rule **never prevents the introduction of evidence that would show that no valid contract exists or that the contract is voidable**.

Illegalität – Täuschung – Zwang – anfechtbar

2. Existence of a Condition

If the parties orally agree on a **condition to the enforceability of the contract**, or to the duty of one of them, but this condition is then not included in the writing, courts generally allow proof of this condition despite the parol evidence rule.

Bedingung

Beweis

3. Collateral Agreements

An oral agreement that is supported by **separate consideration** may be demonstrated, even though it occurred prior to what seems to be a total integration.

mündlich

stattfinden

4. Subsequent Transactions

Recall that the parol evidence rule never bars evidence that after the signing of the writing, the parties orally or in writing agreed to modify or rescind the writing.

aufheben

Part 5: Defenses

A. Introduction

Even where an agreement is supported by valuable consideration or a recognized substitute, contract rights may still be unenforceable because of a defense to formation of the contract, because there is a defect in capacity, or because a defense to enforcement of certain terms exits.

Ersatz

nicht durchsetzbar

B. Defenses to Formation

There are three categories of defenses to formation of a contract:

- absence of mutual assent
- absence of consideration
- illegality

I. Absence of Mutual Assent

Raffles v. Wichelhaus, Court of Exchequer 159 Eng. Rep. 375 (1864)

The plaintiff offered to sell the defendant a certain amount of cotton arriving from Bombay on a ship called the "Peerless". The defendant accepted the offer to take

Baumwolle

shipment and pay within a certain time after arrival of the ship in England. Unfortunately, there were two ships named "Peerless". The one which arrived in October had the cotton, and the defendants refused delivery claiming that when they accepted the offer, they meant that the other ship "Peerless" which was to arrive in December. The plaintiff brought action for breach of contract.

ablehnen, verweigern – Liefe-rung

Vertragsverletzung

Issue

Is the contract void because each of the parties thought that the shipment was coming by a different ship?

Holding and Reasoning

Yes. Where there is mistake of material fact, there is no binding contract. The court reasoned that there was not a "meeting of the minds". To hold the contract binding would be to impose on the defendant a contract different from what he entered into.

Holmes thought that the court was right:

> Oliver W. Holmes (1841–1932)
> Ass. Justice: 1902-1932
> Appointed by: T. Roosevelt

> *"By the theory of our language, while other words mean different things, a proper name means one person or thing and no other. In theory of speech your name men as you and my name means me, and the two names are different. They are different words. In the use of common names and words a plea of different meaning from that adopted by the court would be bad, but here the parties have said different things and never expressed a contract."* [Holmes, The Theory of Legal Interpretation, 12 Harv. L. Rev. 417 (1899)].

II. Absence of Consideration

If the promises exchanged at the formation stage lack the elements of bargain or legal detriment, no contract exists (see supra, page 143)

III. Illegality

In general, if a contract is found to be "illegal," the court will refuse to enforce it.

durchsetzen

1. Kinds of Illegal Contracts

Here are some of the kinds of contracts frequently found to be illegal and thus unenforceable: **"gambling"** or "wagering" contracts, **lending contracts** that violate usury statutes, the pursuit of "maintenance" and "champerty" arrangements by which one person **improperly finances another's lawsuit** and the performance of services without a required license or permit.

spielen – wetten
Wucher

2. Enforceability

As a general rule, neither party to an illegal contract may enforce it. This is not an ironclad rule. In general, contracts that are still wholly executory are less likely to be enforced by the court than those that have been at least partly performed.

eisern

C. Lack of Capacity

I. Infants

An infant is liable for necessaries furnished him, and this liability is quasi-contractual rather than contractual. As a consequence of the quasi-contractual nature of the action, the infant may disaffirm an executory contract for necessaries. Moreover, the infant is **not liable for the contract price**, but for the reasonable value of the necessaries furnished.

Kind – Notwendigkeit
vertragsähnliches Verhältnis
ablehnen – vollstreckend,
ausübend – haftbar
ausstatten

1. Necessaries

The term "necessaries" is **relative to the infant's status in life**. It would seem clear that the range of what is necessary is considerably larger if the infant is emancipated, and larger yet if he is married.

erwachsen

It is obvious that food, shelter, and clothing are necessaries. But the kind of food, shelter, and clothing is another question that is up to the jury. Medical services are necessaries in many instances.
Education is necessary, but the kind of education which is necessary is dependent upon the circumstances of the infant. The same concept applies to business and employment expenses.

Wohnung
Fall

2. Relative Liability

The liability of an infant is relative not only to his status in life but also is dependent upon whether or not he has an existing supply of necessaries, or parents or guardians who are able and willing to supply him with the necessities of life. The mere fact that the goods or services are in general considered necessaries does not make them necessary to the particular infant if he is already supplied with them.

Versorgung – Vormund
erachten

II. Lack of Volitional Consent

Even where a person has the legal capacity to contract, **morally offensive pressure or artifice** exerted by one party against the other may make "consent" to the bargain ineffective.

Fähigkeit
List

1. Duress

Duress is a defense to enforcement of the obligations of a contract. Duress can be committed by violence, imprisonment, wrongful taking and keeping of a person's property, or the threat of any of those acts. **Duress is an action that compels another to do something he would not otherwise do, so there can be no mutual assent when duress is present.** Under some circumstances, a threat to breach a contract unless it is modified in favor of the person making the threat may be duress. The modern rule is that such a threat is duress if the threat would result in irreparable injury and if it is made in "breach of the duty of good faith and fair dealing."

Zwang – Durchsetzbarkeit
Gewalt
Inhaftierung
Drohung
irreparabel

Austin Instrument, Inc. v. Loral Corp., Ct. of Appeals of New York, 272 N.E.2d 533 (1971)

The defendant was under general contract from the government to make radar equipment. The contract had a delivery schedule that provided for liquidated damages for late delivery. They sub-contracted to the plaintiff for a number of high-quality gears. During the performance, the defendant was awarded a second contract, and did not give any of the new business to the plaintiff. According to the defendant, the plaintiff then stopped delivery until the defendant agreed to award all of the second contract needs to plaintiff, as well as pay higher prices retroactively for the first delivery. The defendant claims that they were unable to find any replacement vendor for the gears who could deliver in time, and so were forced to concede to the plaintiff's demands or face damages that would be much greater than the amount they could recover from the plaintiff for breach. The plaintiff is suing for the additional money not yet paid.

Plan – vorsehen – Schadensersatz
Schaltung
zusprechen
Lieferung
rückwirkend
Ersatzverkäufer
gewähren, bewilligen
klagen

Issue

Was the exercise of power by the plaintiff sufficient to be considered to put the defendant under economic duress, thus voiding the modification to the original contract?

Holding and Reasoning

Yes. "A contract is voidable on the ground of duress when it is established that the party making the claim was forced to agree to it by means of a wrongful threat precluding the exercise of his free will."

The court reasoned that the facts supported a finding that the plaintiff was using the fact that they were a key supplier to extort the defendant into paying more money. The majority found that the defendant could not have obtained the parts from any other source, and that the normal remedy of damages for breach in this case would be insufficient because of the clause for liquidated damages for late delivery.

anfechtbar
feststehen
ausschließen
Hauptlieferant
erpressen
Ersatz
unzureichend

Dissent

The dissent reasoned that the facts did not conclusively show economic duress. Austin's version of the story was that there was lack of common understanding as to the specifics of the contract that led to a mutual reformation. They also contended that the delivery stoppage was due to customary vacation period, not an extortion attempt. They also asserted that there were many alternate suppliers that the defendant did not approach.

Mangel
übereinstimmende Veränderung
Ferienzeit – Erpressungsversuch – behaupten – Alternativ angehen, ansprechen

Duress can also consist of **a threat to exercise legal rights** in an oppressive way. An example is an employer who threatens to fire an employee (which the employer has a legal right to do) unless the employee signs an agreement to sell back all shares of stock he has in the company. Under the circumstances, the contract to sell the stock is unenforceable. Where duress is present, the contract is voidable at the option of the victim of the duress. If the contract has already been performed, the victim may recover damages.

Aktien
nicht durchsetzbar
Opfer

2. Undue Influence

"Undue influence" brought to bear by a party to the contract or a third person is a basis for avoiding a contract under certain circumstances. This defense is generally invoked when a **party takes advantage of another's vulnerability to pressure**.

übermäßig
verhindern
erheben
Verletzlichkeit

3. Misrepresentation

A party to a contract that was **procured by misrepresentation or concealment** may avoid the contract. Only misrepresentations of fact, not of opinion, qualify, and the victim of the misrepresentation must have justifiably relied on the misrepresentation. Generally the misrepresentation must have been intentional. But if it concerns a material fact, unintentional misrepresentation may be sufficient.

geschaffen
falsche Darstellung – Verheimlichung
berechtigterweise

Concealment of a fact, rather than the misrepresentation of it, **is tolerated**, because there is generally no duty to disclose anything to the contracting party. But there are several exceptions that result in the party's having a duty to disclose. If one part of the truth is told, but another portion is not, so as to create an overall misleading impression, this non-disclosure may constitute misrepresentation. Positive action taken in concealment, such as sweeping up evidence of termites and painting the affected area just before the sale of a house, can also constitute misrepresentation. Disclosure of a fact is also required where it is needed to prevent some previous assertion from being misleading.
A party who knows that the other is making a mistake as to a basic assumption also has a **duty to disclose**. The party's failure to correct that misunderstanding constitutes a misrepresentation if the non-disclosure amounts to a failure to act in good faith.

Verheimlichung
hinnehmen
aufdecken
irreführen
beseitigen
Termite
Aufdeckung
erfordern
Behauptung
Annahme
betragen, sich belaufen

D. Defenses to Enforcement

There are mainly two different kind of defenses to enforcement:

- Statute of frauds
- unconscionability

The statute of frauds has been discussed before (see supra, page 151).
The concept of unconscionability will be dealt with in another context (see infra, page 187)

Diagram 23

Defenses

Defenses to Formation	Defenses Based on Lack of Capacity	Defenses to Enforcement
1. Absence of mutual assent	1. Contracts with Infants	1. Statute of Frands
2. Absence of consideration	2. Lack of volitional consent	2. Unconscionbility
3. Illegality		

Part 6: Interpretation

Interpretation problems differ from parol evidence rule problems (see supra, page 156) because they involve not terms outside the writing, but determination of the meaning of the terms contained in the writing. The parol evidence rule does not bar the use of **parol evidence to interpret or explain terms** contained in a complete written agreement, but the use of extrinsic evidence to interpret or explain terms may be limited by rules of contract interpretation.

enthalten
hindern, abhalten
äußerlich, fremd

A. Plain Meaning Rule

One approach, called the "plain meaning rule," provides that the meaning of any writing or term which appears to be plain and unambiguous on its face will be determined without using any extrinsic evidence whatsoever. The plain meaning rule does not allow the parties to show what they thought the term meant, and does not even allow evidence of trade usage to interpret the words. Although this rule is widely criticized, "it is undoubtedly still employed frequently or on occasion by the great majority of the jurisdictions in this country."

vorsehen, vorschreiben
unmissverständlich
Handelsbrauch

United States v. Braunstein – 75 F.Supp. 137 (S.D.N.Y., 1947)

The defendant telegrammed a 10 cents/lb bid in response to a request for bids to buy a large amount of raisins from the government. The government's return telegram had a

Gebot

typo which stated that it had accepted the price of 10 cents/box (not 10 cents/lb), and to send payment within 10 days. The defendant did nothing, and 10 days later, when the government realized its error, it sent a follow-up telegram accepting the correct price. The defendant still did nothing, and so government sold the raisins at a loss and sued the defendant for breach of contract.

typo	Tippfehler
accepting	annehmen
loss	Verlust
breach of contract	Vertragsverletzung

Issue

Is there a contract even though the telegram of acceptance had a typo causing the price to be off by 22,000 dollars?

Holding and Reasoning

No. "Since one who speaks or writes, can, by exactness of expression, more easily prevent mistakes in meaning, than one with whom he is dealing, doubts arising from ambiguity of language are resolved against the former in favor of the latter."

The court reasoned that the telegram with the typo did not constitute an agreement because it was ambiguous, and that they had no authority to construct the telegram differently because that would force the parties into a contract, and they would be constructing negotiations instead of constructing a contract that already existed. They further said that a quasi-contract was not applicable here because there was no unjust enrichment.

prevent	hindern
doubts	Zweifel
ambiguity	Mehrdeutigkeit
constitute	darstellen
authority	Macht, Kompetenz
negotiations	Verhandlung
unjust enrichment	ungerechtfertigte Bereicherung

B. Interpretation

I. Parties' Intent

The common law maintains a strong position that terms of a contract should be **interpreted by their external expression** and not by the subjective intentions of one party. Even so, recognizing the importance of the parties' intentions and the imprecisions of language, a more modern approach allows the parties to introduce evidence of what they subjectively thought the terms in the writing meant. Parties may have directly conflicting ideas about what the terms meant. When

maintains	vertreten
external	außenstehend
intentions	Wille
imprecisions	Ungenauigkeit
introduce	einführen

this happens, the court may find that there was no mutual assent and therefore no contract. But if one party knows of or should have known of the meaning attached by the other party to a term, a court will find that there was mutual assent. — anhängen, verbunden sein mit

Fairmount Glass Works v. Crunden-Martin Woodenware Co. – Ct. of App. of Kenntucky, 51 S.W. 196 (1899)

Appellee sent a letter to Appellant asking for a quote on delivery of ten car loads of Mason Jars. Appellant responded with a quote stating prices that would be good if accepted immediately and shipment taken promptly. Appellee then responded by telegram (following up with a letter), ordering ten car loads of jars. Appellant responded that they were all sold out, and refused to book the order. Appellee sued claiming that the contract was closed when they placed the order, and lower court gave judgment accordingly. — Berufungsbeklagter – Berufungskläger – Angebot; ablehnen; klagen

Issue

Is there a contract based on the language that both parties used in their letters?

Holding and Reasoning

Yes. When determining the presence or absence of a contract, the actions of the parties and the meaning of the statements made must be viewed as a whole.

The specific language in the quote was that it was "for immediate acceptance". This can only be construed in the light of the language of the request for quote. It was clear that the buyer wanted to place a specific order, and so when the seller responded with a quote that was for "immediate acceptance", this must be construed as an desire to sell at that price to that buyer. — auslegen; Wunsch

When parties have **conflicting interpretations** of a term in the contract, courts may also make use of some **general principles of law, or maxims** in deciding which interpretation should be followed. The Restatement suggests some of these general principles. — Rechtsgrundsatz

For example, an ambiguous term will be construed **against the drafter** of the agreement. A term that has been negotiated between the parties will control over one that is part of the standardized, non-negotiated part of the contract Another maxim, the primary purpose rule, provides that if the court can determine what the parties' "primary purpose" for making the contract was, that purpose should be given great weight in the interpretation of the terms.

mehrdeutig
Verfasser, Verwender

II. Court-Supplied Terms

Often parties enter into contracts without expressly or implicitly providing all the terms of their agreement. When this occurs courts are often willing to supply the missing term. "When the parties to a bargain sufficiently defined to be a contract have not agreed with respect to a term which is essential to a determination of their rights and duties, **a term which is reasonable in the circumstances is supplied by the courts**."

ausdrücklich
implizit
vorkommen
wesentlich – Rechte – Pflichten
vernünftig

Such court-supplied terms usually deal with an issue that the parties **never even thought about**. A reasonable supplied term is one that the parties would have agreed to or which conforms to commercial standards of fairness.

Frage, Problem
übereinstimmen

Courts are often unwilling to supply certain kinds of missing terms. For example, quantity terms will generally not be filled in, because an objective standard is difficult to find for this usually subjective expectation.

Erwartung

Part 7: Conditions, Performance and Breach

A. Introduction

I. Definition

An event which must occur before a particular performance is due is called a **"condition"** of that performance.
Performance of a contract has been defined generally as the doing of the **acts required by the agreement** at the time and place therefore and in the manner stipulated.

erforderlich
festsetzen

An obligation to perform arises upon the making of a binding contract, even though it is not to be performed until a future date, and the rule is that, for a party to recover upon a contract for nonperformance by the other party, he must establish his own performance, or his offer and ability to perform, or a valid excuse for his failure to perform. It is also a rule that where one party is unable to perform his part of the contract, he cannot be entitled to the performance of the contract by the other party.

entstehen, herausgeben
Nichterfüllung
beanspruchen

Often circumstances make it impractical for parties to tender their performance at the same time. This is the case where the performance of one party will take longer than the other party's. This is especially true of construction contracts where the builder's promised performance is providing a completed building and the owner's performance is payment for that completed building. But under such circumstances the builder can regain the security of simultaneous performance by requesting payments at stated intervals for work completed. It is also very common for one party to tender performance first in reliance on the other party's promise to tender its performance at a later date. This often happens when one party has lesser bargaining power and has no choice but to perform first. This is common when parties have dealt with each other before and one party is willing to perform first.

Bau-
wiedergewinnen – Sicherheit
Vertrauen
schwächere Verhandlungs-position

II. Promise v. Condition

The fact that an act is a condition does not by itself make it also a promise. If the act is a condition on the other party's duty, and the act fails to occur, the other party will not have to perform. If the act is a promise, and it does not occur, the other party can sue for damages. But the two do not automatically go together.

klagen – Schadensersatz

To determine whether a particular act is a condition, a promise, or both, the main factor is the **intent of the parties**. Words like "upon condition that" indicate an intent that the act be a condition; words like "I promise" or "I

Absicht
Bedingung

warrant" indicate a promise (though as described below, failure to keep the promise will also generally constitute the failure of a constructive condition.)

darstellen

1. Express and Implied Conditions

Conditions can be classified in the following manner:

a) Express Conditions

When the parties have agreed to the condition (expressly or impliedly), the condition is an **express condition**. Strict compliance with an express condition is ordinarily required. However, courts often avoid applying the **"strict compliance"** rule where a forfeiture would result. A forfeiture occurs when one party has relied on the bargain (e.g., by preparing to perform or by making part performance), and insistence on strict compliance with the condition would cause him to fail to receive the expected benefits from the deal.

gewöhnlich

Verlust, Einbuße

Bestehen

Despite the rule that strict compliance with an express condition is ordinarily required, the court would probably hold that strict enforcement here would amount to a forfeiture, and would therefore hold that the condition was satisfied despite the trivial defect.

entscheiden

erfüllt, Genüge getan

Alternatively, a court may find that the fulfillment of the express condition is **"excused" where extreme forfeiture would occur**. This will only be done, however, if the damage to the other party's expectations from non-occurrence of the condition is relatively minor. (see, infra, page 176)

Erwartung

b) Implied Conditions

Implied conditions are those fairly to be **inferred from evidence of the parties' intention**; i.e., their existence is determined by the process of contract interpretation. These are usually referred to as "implied in fact" conditions.

Absicht

Taylor v. Caldwell – King's Bench, 122 Eng. Rep. 309 (1863)

The plaintiff wished to put on a show at the defendant's Music Hall. The parties negotiated a written document which contained terms setting forth the various responsibilities of each party. There was no mention made of contingencies in case of destruction of the Music Hall before the show date. The Music Hall burned down a few days before the date through the fault of neither party, and both parties had spent some money in preparation.

enthalten
Verantwortlichkeit
Möglichkeit – Zerstörung
Schuld

Issue
Is the fact that the Music Hall burned down sufficient to absolve the parties from their contractual obligations?

entbinden, lossprechen

Holding and Reasoning
Yes. Where contracting parties do not make explicit representations otherwise, and the nature of the transaction is one in which an objective view of the parties' negotiations shows that they intended not to be bound if the performance became "impossible" due an uncontemplated event, then an "implied condition" is said to exist which excuses the parties from performance upon the happening of the event.
The court reasoned that if the parties had contemplated the burning down of the Music Hall before the performance, they both would have considered themselves not bound. They linked the transaction to one where a painter who was commissioned to paint a work died before it was finished, thus releasing him from his obligation.

Ausführung
unvorhersehbar – stillschweigend vereinbarte Bedingung – Entschuldigung
befreien, erlassen

2. Constructive Condition

A promise might not be expressly conditional on performance by the other party. In the absence of the doctrine of "constructive conditions," a party would be obligated to perform his promise even though the other party has not performed. Beginning in the 18th century,

Fehlen

courts recognized the seeming unfairness of a party who was in breach of a contract <u>suing</u> to enforce the other party's performance. In response, courts began to <u>imply</u> conditions into agreements where the parties have not expressly agreed otherwise.

klagen
hineinlesen

a) General Rule

Where each party makes one or more <u>promises</u> to the other, each party's substantial performance of his promise is generally a constructive condition to the performance of any subsequent <u>duties</u> by the other party.

Versprechen
Pflicht

b) Order of Performance

One has to be careful to interpret the contract to determine the order in which the parties' performances are to occur.

- **Intent:** The parties' intent always controls. Where the intent is not clear, the court supplies certain <u>presumptions</u>, as discussed below.

Annahme

- **Periodic alternating:** The parties may agree that their performances shall <u>alternate</u>. This is true of most <u>installment</u> contracts. Here, a series of alternating constructive conditions arises: each party's obligation to perform his duty is constructively conditioned on the other's having performed the prior duty. It's therefore important to decide who was the first to fail to substantially perform, since that failure of substantial performance is the non-occurrence of a constructive condition of the other party's <u>subsequent</u> duty.

wechseln
Raten
nachfolgend

- **No order of performance agreed upon:** If the parties do not agree upon the order of performance, there are several general <u>presumptions</u> courts use:
  - Only one party's work requires time: Where the performance of one party requires a period of time, and the other's does not, the performance requiring time must ordinarily <u>occur</u> first, and its performance is a constructive condition to the other party's performance.

Vermutung
stattfinden

This applies to contracts for services – a party who is to perform work must usually substantially complete the work before he may receive payment if the parties do not otherwise agree.

B. Independent or Dependent Promises

In the normal bilateral contract, the court will presume that the promises are in exchange for each other. That is, the court will treat the **promises as being mutually dependent**, so that each party's duty is constructively conditional upon the other's substantial performance of all previous duties.

zweiseitig

I. Independent Promises

But in a few situations, circumstances may indicate that the promises are intended to be independent of each other. Here, the court will not apply the theory of constructive conditions.

unabhängig

For instance, promises in the typical real estate lease are generally construed as being independent of each other. Thus a tenant's promise to pay rent, and a landlord's return-promise to make repairs, are treated as independent, so if the landlord does not make the repairs, the tenant cannot refuse to pay the rent (though he can of course sue for damages). But a growing minority of courts have rejected this rule of independence.

Grundstücksmiete
auslegen
Mieter – Mietzins – Vermieter

II. Classification According to Time of Occurrence

Furthermore, conditions can be classified according to the time of their occurrence:

1. Conditions Precedent

A **condition precedent** is one that must occur before an absolute duty of immediate performance arises in the other party.

vorhergehend

2. Conditions Concurrent

Conditions concurrent are those that are capable of occurring together, and the parties are bound to perform at the same time. Thus, in effect, each is a condition "precedent" to the other.

zeitgleich – fähig

3. Conditions Subsequent

A **condition subsequent** is one the occurrence of which cuts off an already existing absolute duty of performance.

nachfolgend

4. Distinction

The distinction between a condition precedent and subsequent is important only in regard to **burdens of pleading and proof**.
The plaintiff must usually plead and prove the condition precedent because he claims there is a duty to be performed. The defendant must usually plead and prove a condition subsequent because he claims the duty that existed no longer exists.

Darlegungs- und Beweislast

III. Presumption Against Forfeiture

If one party does not have to perform because a condition has not occurred and the other party has performed or has otherwise relied substantially on the contract, **the performing party will be denied compensation**. This resulting denial of compensation is called "forfeiture." This is a harsh result, so courts usually try to avoid forfeiture using various methods. Where possible, a court might interpret the contract language so as not to impose a condition. If there is clearly a condition, and it appears that forfeiture may result, the court might avoid the forfeiture by concluding that the condition has been satisfied.

stattfinden
Ersatz
Verlust
auslegen
folgern

IV. Excuse of Conditions

A party can be excused from not performing conditions if the other party's wrongful conduct prevented performance of the condition. When performance of the condition is excused, the other party, whose performance was conditional, must perform notwithstanding the fact that the condition was not performed.

entschuldigen
hindern
unabhängig von

C. Sufficiency of Performance

I. In General

A party to a contract should **perform stipulations strictly or literally**, but at least substantially, before he is entitled to the performance of the promise made by the other party or to damages for a nonperformance. However, a person cannot be compelled to take and use one thing when he bargained for another and declines to receive the substitute tendered. He has the right to have the thing contracted for in the form agreed upon and cannot be put off with something different even though, in a strict pecuniary sense, it is more valuable.

zwingen
erhalten – Ersatz
geldlich

What constitutes full performance generally depends upon a construction of the contract in light of what has been done in carrying it out. Strict or full performance may, of course, be waived. And one may recover, under a contract to do certain work, on performance thereof jointly with another, unless the contract was for his personal advice.

Ersatz erhalten
gemeinsam
persönlicher Rat

II. Substantial Performance

The Doctrine

The doctrine of substantial performance looks at the **spirit of the contract** and not at the letter of it, and the question therefore is not whether a party has literally complied with it, but whether he has substantially done so. This has long been the rule in equity. The performing party is not absolutely free from fault or omission in every particular case, but he will not be turned away in court if he has in good faith made substantial performance.

Geist
Wortlaut
Billigkeitsrecht
Unterlassung, Versäumnis

Where one party to a contract has received the benefits of a substantial partial performance of the agreement by the other party who has not fully performed all his contractual promises, the first party cannot retain the benefits and repudiate the burdens of the contract, but he is bound to perform his part of the agreement and his remedy for the breach is limited to compensation in damages.

Vorteil

Vertragsversprechen

III. Suspension Followed by Discharge

If a party fails to substantially perform, but the defects could be fairly easily cured, **the other party's duty to give a return performance is merely suspended**; the defaulter then has a chance to cure his defective performance. If, on the other hand, the defect is so substantial that it cannot be cured within a reasonable time, or if the defaulter fails to take advantage of a chance to cure, the other party is then completely discharged, and may also sue for breach.

Mangel
heilen
aussetzen

angenommen

IV. Factors Regarding Materiality

Here are some factors that help determine whether a breach is material (i.e., whether the breaching party has nonetheless substantially performed):

feststellen
erheblich

1. Deprivation of Expected Benefit

The more the non-breaching party is **deprived of the benefit** which he reasonably expected, the more likely it is that the breach was material.

entziehen
wahrscheinlich

2. Part Performance

The greater the part of the performance which has been rendered, the less likely it is that a breach will be deemed material. Thus a breach occurring at the very beginning of the contract is more likely to be deemed material than the same "size" breach coming near the end.

erbringen – erachten

3. Likeliness of Cure

If the breaching party seems likely to be able and willing to cure, the breach is less likely to be material than where **cure seems impossible**.

bereit sein

4. Willfulness

A willful (i.e., intentional) breach is more likely to be regarded as material than a breach caused by negligence or other factors.

5. Delay

A delay, even a substantial one, will not necessarily constitute a lack of substantial performance. The presumption is that **time is not "of the essence"** unless the contract so states, or other circumstances make the need for promptness apparent.

Verzögerung
Fehlen

a) General Rule

It is a general rule that one who contracts to complete certain work within a certain time is **liable** for the damage **for not completing it within such time**, unless the delay is excused or waived. Thus, even though time is not of the specified time, he is liable in damages for the delay. However, the noncompletion of performance within the time specified by the contract will not forfeit a right to recover the contract price where the contract provides for liquidated damages to be deducted from the price in case performance is not completed within the specified time; in such a case failure to complete within a fixed period does not forfeit the right to recover for work already done at the date fixed for completion or yet to be done at that time. Nor will a demonstrated inability by one party complete a building on or before a time specified justify the other party in repudiating, in advance, an agreement to make a certain loan upon completion of the building by such specified time where that time is not of the essence of the agreement.

haftbar – Schaden
Nichterfüllung
verwirken
abziehen
rechtfertigen
zurückweisen

b) Excuses and Waivers

Excuses for delay from causes beyond the control of the contractor would seem to be governed by the same rules as excuses for nonperformance. Also an **Act of God will excuse** a delay in performance.	Entschuldigung Vertragspartei in etwa: höhere Gewalt
Rights arising form delay in performance **may be waived**. Where time is of the essence, a breach of the contract in that respect by one of the parties may be waived by the other party's subsequently treating the contract as still in force. The validity of the waiver requires that it shall be made intentionally and voluntarily.	verzichten Wirksamkeit absichtlich – freiwillig

V. Partial Performance

The general rule is that partial performance of an entire and indivisible contract by one of the parties does not entitle him to performance of the contract by the other or to a recovery against the other on the contract. This rule has many exceptions developed by the equity courts when equitable circumstances intervened.	gesamt, vollständig berechtigen eingreifen

Britton v. Turner – S. Ct. of Judicature of New Hampshire, 6 N.H. 481 (1834)

The plaintiff was a hired hand working for the defendant under a 1 year employment contract. The plaintiff quit working for the defendant before the end of the year, and the defendant therefore refused to pay him any part of his salary, claiming that the plaintiff breached the contract, and so he was discharged from his performance.	gemietet aufhören Lohn befreit

Issue

Is the defendant liable for payment of the value of the partial performance even though the plaintiff breached the express contract?

Holding and Reasoning

Yes. Where a person has only partially performed a contract, and the contract does not explicitly state that payment will not be tendered for anything less than	leisten

complete performance, the benefiting party is liable for the value of the performance to the extent that 1) he benefited from the partial performances, and 2) he has accepted the performance.

The court reasoned that it would be unjust for the employer not to pay for the benefit he received. The common understanding of the hired-hand employment contract is that the employee is entitled for compensation for services actually performed, even if the contract is not completed. Otherwise, an employer would be motivated to try and convince the employee to quit near the end of his term. This presumption can be contracted out of only by specific and express language to the contrary.

ungerecht
Arbeitgeber
Angestellter
Annahme

1. Inability to Complete

Where a default is clearly not willful or deliberate, but the result of **circumstances beyond the defaulter's control**, and there is a substantial and unjust enrichment of the other party by the defaulter's partial performance, there may be recovery for such performance over and above the actual damages caused by the default.

The prevention, by the Act of God, of full performance of an entire contract will permit a recovery upon an implied obligation for personal services already rendered in part performance of the contract.

bewusst, vorsätzlich
ungerechtfertigte Bereicherung
in etwa: höhere Gewalt

2. Illness or Death

As a general rule, **recovery** may be had **for the value of the services actually rendered** where the performance of an entire contract for personal services is prevented by sickness or death. A circumstance that has had a decisive influence in this respect is the fact that in such case the other party has received and retains the benefit of the services. It is not just that one should benefit by the labor of another and make no return when the event which ends the service happens without the fault of either party and is not expressly or impliedly stipulated against in the agreement which induced

abhalten, verhindern
nutzen
vereinbaren

the labor. However, even though a failure to perform fully is caused by death or sickness, there can be no recovery upon the contract for a partial performance of an indivisible contract if the failure of performance is a substantial failure of consideration and there is no provision in the contract to the contrary.

untrennbar

3. Destruction of Subject Matter

Where the subject matter of a contract is destroyed without fault on the part of the promisor, rendering full performance impossible, it has been held that he may recover for so much of the undertaking as he has already performed, at least if the promisee has been benefited thereby.
However, in case of the destruction of the fruits of services, so that neither party has the value of them, the loss must generally be adjusted according to the nature and scope of the contract and the circumstances of the case.

Gegenstand
Versprechender
Versprechensempfänger
Zerstörung

D. Waiver of Strict or Full Performance

Strict and full performance of a contract by one party may be waived by the other party, in which case there is, to the extent of the waiver, no right to damages for the failure to perform strictly and fully. This is in accord with the elementary general principle that **either party to a contract may waive any of the provisions made for his benefit**. Departures from the contract as to quantities and as to point of delivery may be waived. A defense that work was not properly done may also be waived, and there may be a mutual estoppel, by waiver, as to effect of a default.
Subject to the qualification that to be effectual a waiver of a stipulation in an agreement must not only be made intentionally, but with knowledge of the circumstances, contract provisions may be waived expressly or the waiver thereof may be implied from the acts of the parties. Sometimes waiver is proved by the express declaration of a party or by his undisputed acts or language so inconsistent with a purpose to stand on the contract provisions as to leave no opportunity for a reasonable inference to the contrary, in which case the waiver is established as a matter of law.

verzichten
Schadensersatzanspruch
in Übereinstimmung mit
zu seinen Gunsten
Abweichung
„Hemmung“ – Verzicht
Auflage, Bedingung
ausdrückliche Erklärung
unstreitig – widersprüchlich
Gelegenheit – (Schluss-) Folgerung

E. Excuses for Nonperformance

I. Mistake

A party may be released from a contract if the **contract was based upon a mutual mistake**, and he did not bear the risk of that mistake. The mistake must concern a **basic assumption** on which the contract was made, such as the nature, identity, or existence of the subject matter.
For example, if a non-farmer sees what he believes to be a cow and agrees to buy it, but it is actually a steer, the buyer will still have to perform. **The mistake here was not mutual**; it was unilateral. Also, the buyer bore the risk of this mistake, since he knew that his knowledge was incomplete, but chose to proceed anyway. On the other hand, if two parties agree to the sale of the cow, but neither of them knew that the cow had died before their agreement, the **mistake is mutual** and the seller will not have to perform.

entbinden, befreien
tragen
Annahme
Stier
einseitig – tragen
beidseitig

Sherwood v. Walker – 33 N.W. 919 (Mich. 1887)

The plaintiff desired to purchase a cow of distinguished ancestry named Rose 2d of Aberlone from the defendant. The plaintiff went to defendant's farm and found a cow he wished to purchase, and the defendant agreed to sell Rose to the plaintiff for 5 1/2 ¢ per lb in writing. Rose went for US$ 80 because both parties believed that she was sterile. The defendant gave the plaintiff an order directing the farm to deliver cow to the plaintiff. The defendant realized before delivery to the plaintiff that the cow was pregnant, and therefore worth between US$ 750 and 1000, and refused to deliver the cow to the plaintiff. The plaintiff tendered agreed upon price to defendant, and then filed suit.

ausgezeichnet
Stammbaum
kaufen
Auftrag
schwanger
ablehnen, verweigern
Klage erheben

Issue
Did the fact that the cow was actually pregnant mean that the cow was not actually the "thing bargained for", thus meaning there was no contract?

Holding and Reasoning

Yes. A person who makes a contract may rescind if the contract was made upon the mistake of fact that induced the agreement.

aufheben, zurücktreten
veranlassen, herbeiführen

The parties would not have made the contract except that both thought the cow to be barren, which amounts to mistake of material fact.

unfruchtbar

Dissent

The defendant made the mistake, under his own judgment, "without any common understanding with the other party in the premises as to the quality of the animal", and is therefore remediless.

Gelände, Grundstück
ohne Anspruch

II. Changed Circumstances: Impossibility and Frustration of Purpose

1. Impossibility

A party might also be released from a contract where, through no fault of the parties, the **performance** has become **impossible** or the principal purpose of one of the parties in **entering into the contract has become frustrated**.

entbinden, befreien
Schuld
vereiteln, zunichte machen

Fibrosa Spolka Akcyjna v. Fairbairn Lawson Combe Barbour, Ltd. – 144 A.L.R. 1298 (1943)

The plaintiff is a Polish company who expressly contracted with the defendant to buy some machines and have them delivered to Poland. They were supposed to have made a down payment of 1/3 upon order, but paid somewhat less than that. The defendant began the construction of the machines. Poland was subsequently invaded by Germany, which made it impossible to deliver the machines. The plaintiff sued to get his down payment back.

Anzahlung
Bau, Erstellung

Issue

Is the subsequent impossibility of performance by the defendant sufficient to release the parties from further contractual liability, as well as entitle the plaintiff to

nachfolgend
ausreichend
Haftung

recover any down payment, even though the defendant had already gone to some expenditure to make the machines? — Aufwand, Ausgaben

Holding and Reasoning

Yes. Where the performance of a contract has begun, but further performance of a contract becomes impossible due to events unanticipated (unvorhersehbar) by the parties and beyond their control, the contract fails for lack of consideration, and any partial payment by the buyer is refundable (erstatten, ersetzen). The court expressly overruled *Chandler v. Webster*, and claimed that the plaintiff was entitled to recovery, not by release by implied condition, but that failure of consideration prevented the contract from being formed at all. The court reasoned that the contract was for delivery, and so when delivery became impossible, the whole contract failed for lack of consideration. Thus, they awarded restitution damages to the plaintiff on a theory of quasi-contract (vertragsähnliches Verhältnis) because the whole contract had failed.

2. Impracticability

In some cases, the performance has not become literally impossible, but unforeseeable (unvorhersehbar) circumstances have made **performance extremely costly or burdensome** (belastend). This is known as "impracticability," and the modern trend is release a party from a contract if performance becomes extremely impracticable. But impracticality requires (erfordern) that the economic loss be both substantial and unforeseen at the time the contract was made. Many of the modern cases dealing with impracticability have involved drastic increases (Steigerung) in energy costs resulting from the oil embargo of the 1970s. These cases show that courts are generally unwilling (nicht bereit sein) to release parties from their obligations (Verpflichtung) simply because of lost profits.

American Trading and Production Corp. v. Shell International Marine, Ltd. – 453 F.2d 939 (2d Cir. 1972)

The plaintiff is the owner of a cargo ship (Frachtschiff). The defendant is the charterer of the cargo ship. The charterer and the owner negotiated a price to transport and deliver some cargo from Texas to India. During transit, the Suez Canal became closed because of war in the Mideast. The owner was forced to take the Cape of Good Hope route to India, and thus incurred extra costs. The plaintiff is suing for the extra costs incurred on the theory of commercial impracticability of the contract which excused him from performance, and entitled him to reimbursement for the added costs incurred.

zwingen – Kap der guten Hoffnung
entstehen
Erstattung

Issue
Is the closing of the canal a condition upon which the contract was grounded, thus causing frustration when the canal was closed? Did the closing of the canal result in commercial impracticability?

basieren

Holding and Reasoning
No. Expectation that the parties will be able to profit from a contract does not make profitability a condition of performance. Mere increase in cost alone is not a sufficient excuse for non-performance; it must be an "extreme and unreasonable" expense.
The court reasoned that although the parties expected that the canal would be used, the cape route was an acceptable alternative. The fact that the parties negotiated a price based on the going rate for the Suez crossing does not mean that the openness of the Suez Canal was a condition of the contract. The owner made an unconditional promise of delivery to the charterer. Also, the additional cost incurred was only 30% more than the contract price, so the loss was not extreme.

Steigerung
übertrieben, unzumutbar
annehmbar
unbedingt, bedingungslos

3. Frustration of Purpose

Frustration of purpose occurs when the purpose of the contract has been unexpectedly destroyed.

stattfinden, vorliegen

Krell v. Henry – Court of App., 2 K.B. 740 (1903)

The plaintiff owned a room which had windows that looked out over the area where the King Edward's VII coronation was to take place, and put up signs in his window offering the use of the rooms for people to watch the coronation. The defendant paid a down payment to use a room for the days of the coronation, but the King became sick and was unable to be coronated. The defendant refused to pay the balance of the money for the room, and the plaintiff brought this suit.

Krönung
Anzahlung
ablehnen – Differenz, Restbetrag

Issue
Is the fact that the coronation did not take place sufficient to release the parties from their contractual obligations?

Holding and Reasoning
Yes. Where from the nature of the contract, it can be objectively determined from the parties' conduct that both parties meant to be released from liability upon the failure of a certain event to happen, even if it is not expressly stated by the parties, it is an implied condition of the contract.
The court reasoned that the "foundation" of the contract was that the room could be used to view the coronation. Thus, the happening of the coronation was an implied condition of the contract. They reasoned that the non-happening of the coronation was of such a character that it cannot reasonably be supposed to have been in the contemplation of the contracting parties when the contract was made.

Verhalten
Haftung
stillschweigend vereinbarte Bedingung – Grundlage
annehmen
Erwägung

The foregoing decision is the best-known example of the doctrine of **"frustration of purpose"**. As opposed to impossibility, the label frustration signifies that nothing has happened to impede performance of the defendant's undertaking. After the King's illness, as before, it was perfectly possible to pay the agreed price – and indeed to occupy the rooms.

bedeuten
hindern, erschweren

4. Reformation of Contracts

Instead of declaring the contract invalid because of changed circumstances, a court may try to "reform" it. However, **U.S. courts generally feel that they have no power to**

ändern, verbessern

impose unbargained-for terms upon parties. Such action is seen as a direct interference with a free market and the right to contract freely. This is based on the view that a contract is an agreement that parties enter to guarantee their own expectations. Therefore it is the expectations of the parties that the common law court seeks to enforce. One can nonetheless find occasional **cases where contracts have been reformed**.

nicht in die Verhandlung einbezogen

Erwartung
durchsetzen

5. Unconscionability

A party may be excused from performance under a contract if the contract is found to be **unconscionable**. A contract may be unconscionable if there was an **absence of meaningful choice on** the part of one of the parties together with contract terms which are unreasonably favorable to the other party.

skrupellos, unverschämt

günstig

A burdensome clause that does not come to the attention of a party adhering to a contract will be struck down if a **reasonable person would not expect to find it in the contract** and the reason it was not noticed was its burial in small print, or the inability of the adhering party to comprehend the language.

belastend
haften, festhalten – ungültig erklären
Begräbnis
Kleingedrucktes – festhalten

Provisions of a contract that are assented to but are grossly one-sided may be invalidated or modified by the court. A contract that suffers from total overall imbalance, that is, one that is grossly one-sided, may be invalidated.

zustimmen
ungültig machen

Although analytically the surprise and oppression cases can be distinguished, in general, where unconscionability has been found, the facts contain a mixture of lack of knowledgeable assent and a clause or contract that unduly benefits the party who has drafted it

United States v. Bethlehem Steel Corp., 315 U.S. 289 (1952)

During World War I, the U.S. needed ships built quickly. The defendant offered to build the ships for a cost-plus-fixed-fee contract with a savings-clause to reward them 50% of the money that they saved over the estimated cost. They set the cost estimates very high to assure themselves

Schätzung – sichern

a profit, and the U.S. felt that they had no choice but to go along because they were in such a bad position. Upon completion of the ships, the U.S. refused to pay the total amount of the savings clause.

Issue

Is the relationship between the United States and the defendant so lopsided that it would render the contract "unconscionable" and unenforceable? — schief, einseitig

Holding and Reasoning

No. A contract is enforceable when it is made with the full recognition of the risks by both parties, and there is no fraud. — Täuschung

The majority reasoned that although the U.S. resented the greediness of the defendant, they made the contract with their "eyes open", and therefore the express contract should be enforced. — Gier

Dissent

The dissent reasoned that there was not an opportunity to reach a just result because of the extreme lopsidedness of the bargaining power of each side. The need of the government was extremely urgent, and they were faced with either agreeing to the defendant's terms or commandeering the plant and building the ships themselves. Whenever one party can dictate all the terms of the contract, and the other must acquiesce, it is coercion. They further reasoned that the defendant took no risk of loss because of the cost-plus-fixed-fee contract. — Gelegenheit; Verhandlungsmacht; eilig, dringend; leiten, befehlen; einwilligen; Zwang

Unconscionability often arises as a result of **standardized contracts**, which are now commonly used in many types of transactions. Often parties signing these contracts, especially private consumers, are unaware of the meaning of the terms contained or are unable to negotiate the terms because of an unequal bargaining power. The **U.C.C.** does provide for the obligation of good faith in all contracts and for the removal of unconscionable terms. However, it must be remembered that the U.C.C. applies only to contracts for the sales of goods (see infra, chapter 4, volume 2). — vorliegen, aufkommen; Verbraucher – nicht bemerken; verhandeln

Patterson v. Walker-Thomas Furniture Co., 277 A.2d 111 (DC 1971)

Appellant put merchandise on layaway, and then failed to pay all of the installments. The Appellee sued for the balance, to which the appellant responded that they were grossly over-priced, and therefore the contract should be negated due to unconscionability. The appellant wished to have the court subpoena the invoices of the appellee to show that she was over-charged based on what they paid.

Berufungskläger – Ware – angezahlt – Rate – Berufungsbeklagter

erzwingen – Rechnung

Issue

Is there sufficient evidence to show unconscionability and void the contract?

Holding and Reasoning

No. "[T]wo elements are required to exist to prove unconscionability; i.e., an absence of meaningful choice on the part of one of the parties together with contract terms which are unreasonably favorable to the other party".

The court reasoned that the appellant provided no evidence that she had an absence of meaningful choice. Therefore, there was no reason to investigate the validity of the price by subpoena of the appellee's invoices.

Beweis

untersuchen

6. Difficulty, Hardship, or Financial Loss

As a general principle, difficulty or even improbability of accomplishment without **financial loss will not release a party from his contract**. Many cases hold that inconvenience or the cost of compliance, though they might make compliance a hardship, cannot excuse a party from the performance of an absolute and unqualified undertaking to do a thing that is possible and lawful, inasmuch as parties sui juris bind themselves by their lawful contracts, and courts cannot alter them because they work a hardship. The rights of the parties must be measured by the contract which they themselves made, and a contract is not invalid, nor is the obligor therein in any manner discharged from its binding effect, because it turns out to be difficult or

Unwahrscheinlichkeit

Erreichung

Unbequemlichkeit – Einwilligung

Unternehmen

Härte

Verpflichteter

burdensome to perform. It has been said that difficulties, even if unforeseen and however great, are no excuse, and that the fact that a contract has become increasingly difficult and expensive to perform because of a law enacted after its execution does not excuse performance. — verrichten

Part 8: Remedies

A. Damages

The basic goal of contract damages is to **compensate the aggrieved party** with enough money to attain the same economic position that would have been attained if the contract had been fully performed. The aggrieved party is entitled to the "benefit of the bargain," receiving "gains prevented" (expectancy interest) plus "losses sustained" (reliance and restitutionary interests), subject to the limitations imposed by the doctrines of foreseeability, certainty, and mitigation.

ausgleichen
belasten
Erwartungs-
Vertrauen – Erstattungs-
Vorhersehbarkeit

I. General Principles

1. Foreseeability

Contract damages cannot be recovered unless they were **foreseeable to the parties at the time of contracting**. "General Damages" are those foreseeable to reasonable persons similarly situated and are calculated by the standardized rules discussed below. **"Special"** or **"consequential"** damages are those that are foreseeable because, at the time of contracting, the party in breach knows that in the event of breach no substitute performance will be available.

wiedererlangen
berechnen

2. Certainty

The plaintiff may only recover for losses which he establishes with "reasonable certainty." Mainly, this means that a plaintiff who claims that he would have made profits had the defendant not breached must show not only that there would have been profits, but also the likely **amount of those profits**.

wahrscheinlich

a) Profits From a New Business

Courts are especially reluctant to award lost profits from a new business, that is, a business which at the time of breach was not yet in actual operation. — zögerlich

b) Cost of Completion Unknown

Also, the "reasonable certainty" requirement may fail to be met where the plaintiff cannot show accurately enough what his cost of completion would have been. — Erfordernis; genau

3. Mitigation

Damages that could have been avoided by reasonable efforts cannot be recovered. Conversely, the aggrieved party may recover reasonable costs **incurred in an effort to minimize damages**. — Anstrengung; umgekehrt – belastet; erleiden, aufwenden

One is not required to enter into another contract with the breaching party even if the offered contract would have minimized damages. — Schaden

The principle of mitigation is not necessarily applicable in cases where the relationship between the parties is not exclusive. If the aggrieved party is free to enter into other similar contracts, entry into such a contract after breach does not reduce the damages that may be recovered. — Milderung; mindern

II. Types

1. Expectation Damages

In most breach of contract cases, the plaintiff will seek, and receive, protection for his **"expectation interest."** Here, the court attempts to put the plaintiff in the position he would have been in had the contract been performed. In other words, the plaintiff is given the "benefit of his bargain," including any profits he would have made from the contract. — Schutz; versuchen; durchführen, erfüllen

Expectation damages are the usual measure of damages for breach of contract. The court tries to put the plaintiff in the **position he would have been in had the contract been performed by the defendant**. The plaintiff should end up with a sum equal to his costs already incurred, plus the profit he would have made had the contract been completed.

Gewinn

2. Formula for Calculating

Plaintiff's expectation damages are equal to the value of the defendant's promised performance (generally the contract price), minus whatever benefits the plaintiff has received from not having to complete his own performance. The plaintiff's cost of completion (the amount he has saved by not having to finish) does not include any part of his overhead.

Wert
versprochen
Vorteil
laufende Geschäftskosten

Where defendant has defectively performed, plaintiff normally can recover the **cost of remedying defendant's defective performance**. But if the cost of remedying defects is clearly disproportionate to the loss in market value from the defective performance, plaintiff will only recover the **loss in market value**.

fehlerhaft
wiedererlangen

The "principle of economic waste" is often applied where the defect is minor, and remedying it would involve "economic waste", such as the destruction of what has already been done.

gering
Zerstörung

Jacob & Youngs, Inc. v. Kent – Ct. of App. of New York, 129 N.E. 889 (1921)

The plaintiff built a house for the defendant. The contract specification called for wrought iron pipe made by Reading. The plaintiff's subcontractor delivered Reading pipe for the first 1,000 feet of pipe, but thereafter delivered pipe from other manufacturers. When the building was completed, the defendant took possession and noticed that the pipe was not made by Reading. The plaintiff's architect refused to sign off the final certificate, and the plaintiff withheld payment. There was evidence that the pipe actually used was of the same quality as Reading pipe, and that the cost of replacing the entire plumbing with the Reading pipe would have been exorbitant because it would have required rebuilding the house.

Schmiedeeisen – Leitung, Rohr
Hersteller
ablehnen
zurückhalten, verweigern – Beweis
ersetzen – Rohrleitungen
astronomisch, exorbitant

Issue

Is the omission of Reading pipe in the house a cause for forfeiture of the final contract payment?

Unterlassen, Versäumnis
Verwirkung

Holding and Reasoning

No. An omission which is trivial and innocent does not necessarily result in a forfeiture, but rather may be remedied by the payment of damages.

unschuldig

The majority [Cardozo] reasoned that the omission of the pipe was not willful, and furthermore, there was evidence that the pipe actually used was of the same quality. The brand name of the pipe was not crucial to the building of the house, and it would be extremely burdensome on the plaintiff to require him to rebuild the plumbing. Although the plaintiff could not simply substitute his own judgment for what is stipulated in the contract, the deviation was so minor as to be considered a covenant and not a condition. The measure of damages, therefore, was not the price of installing new plumbing, but rather the difference in value between what was actually installed and the Reading pipes.

Benjamin N. Cardozo (1870–1938)
Ass. Justice: 1932-1938
Appointed by: H. Hoover

Markenname – entscheidend

ersetzen
Abweichung
Zusicherung, Verpflichtung

Dissent

The dissent [McLaughlin] stated that the defendant was entitled to exactly the kind of pipe that was stated in the contract, whether the other kind was just as good, even if it was simply a whim. The dissent concluded that the deviation was not innocent, and whether it was intentional or unintentional, it should be treated as intentional because it was careless. Otherwise, parties would be motivated to deviate from contracts intentionally, and the law would suffer.

berechtigt

Laune

sorglos
leiden

3. Reliance Damages

Reliance damages are the damages needed to put the plaintiff in the position he would have been in had the **contract never been made**. Therefore, these damages usually equal the amount the plaintiff has spent in performing or in preparing to perform. They are used either where there is a contract but expectation damages cannot be accurately calculated, or where there is no contract but some relief is justifiable. — Ersatz – gerechtfertigt

4. Nominal Damages

Where a right of action for breach exists, but no harm has been done or is provable, the plaintiff may get a judgment for **nominal damages**. That is, he may recover a small **sum that is fixed without regard to the amount of harm he has suffered**. — beweisbar

5. Punitive Damages

Punitive damages are **rarely awarded** in breach of contract cases. But if the breach of contract also constitutes a tort, punitive damages are recoverable. Many courts now regard a party's bad faith conduct in connection with a contract as being itself a tort, for which punitive damages may be awarded. For instance, if a party breaches voluntarily, in order to make a better deal elsewhere, the court may find that this conduct constitutes bad faith punishable by punitive damages. — Strafschadensersatz – zusprechen – Delikt; böser Glaube; freiwillig

6. Liquidated Damages

A "liquidated damages clause" is a **contractual provision** that determines in advance the measure of damages to be assessed if a party defaults. — Vertragsbestimmung; festsetzen

Courts will enforce liquidated damages provisions, but only if the court is satisfied that the provision is not a "penalty". That is, the court wants to be satisfied that the clause really is an attempt to estimate actual damages, rather than to penalize the party for breach by awarding "damages" that are far in excess of the ones actually suffered. — Strafe

All courts refuse to enforce liquidated damages clauses that do not provide for a "reasonable" amount. This means that a clause which is an unreasonable forecast (viewed as of the time of contracting) can still be saved if it turns out that — Vorhersage plaintiff's damages are unexpectedly high, and therefore in line with the clause.

B. Restitution

The plaintiff's restitution interest is defined as the value to the defendant of the plaintiff's performance. Restitution's goal is to prevent unjust enrichment.
The main uses of the **restitution measure** are as follows:

Rückerstattung
ungerechtfertigte Bereicherung

- a **non-breaching plaintiff** who has partly performed before the other party breached may bring suit on the contract, and not be limited by the contract price (as he would be for the expectation and reliance measures); and
- a **breaching plaintiff** who has not substantially performed may bring a quasi-contract suit and recover the value that he has conferred upon the defendant.

Klage
beschränkt
verleihen

I. Market Value

Restitution is based on the value rendered to the defendant, regardless of how much the conferring of that value costs the plaintiff and regardless of how much the plaintiff was injured by the defendant's breach. This value is usually the **sum which the defendant would have to pay to acquire the plaintiff's performance**, not the subjective value to the defendant.

verleihen
erwerben

II. Not Limited to the Contract Price

The main use of the restitution measure is that, in most courts, it is not limited by the contract price. If the work done by the plaintiff prior to defendant's breach has already enriched the defendant in an amount greater than the contract price, this entire enrichment may be recovered by the plaintiff. This makes restitution sometimes very attractive, compared with both reliance and expectation measures.

Vertragspreis
vor
bereichern
gesamt

III. Losing Contract

Restitution may even be awarded where the plaintiff has partly performed, and would have lost money had the contract been completed.

teilweise erfüllen

C. Equitable Remedies

Sometimes the court will award **"equitable remedies"** instead of the usual remedy of money damages. There are two types of equitable relief relevant to contract cases:

Billigkeitsrechtsfolgen

- **specific performance**
- **injunctions**.

I. Specific Performance

Equity will enforce a contract by decreeing specific performance or by a restraining order only **if the legal remedy of damages or restitution is inadequate**. A decree for specific performance orders the promisor to render the promised performance.

verfügen, erlassen
einstweilige Verfügung
unangemessen
verpflichten – leisten

Stokes v. Moore – 77 So. 2d 331 (1955)

Stokes was hired by Moore to manage their finance company in Mobile. The employment contract stipulated that if Stokes were to leave the employment of Moore at any time, that he could not work in the finance business in Mobile for a period of one year. Furthermore, he was to pay $500 liquidated damages for each breach. After 4 years of employment, Stokes left Moore's company and formed his own competing company, actively soliciting the business of his former clients. Moore brought this action for breach to enforce the injunction term of the employment contract.

mieten
versehen

Wettbewerb – bitten um
früherer

Issue

Is a term in a contract that explicitly requires specific performance of the contract binding simply because it is expressly provided as a remedy? — erfordern

Holding and Reasoning

No. Although the presence of a specific performance clause is a factor the court must consider in making an equitable remedy, it is not determinative. — zwingend

The court reasoned that an injunction was a discretionary tool of the court to prevent substantial injury when no adequate monetary remedy was available. Since the contract provided for liquidated damages, as well as an injunction, the court could consider doing both. However, it was not bound by the contract to automatically grant an injunction since breach was shown. In this case, the court noted that liquidated damages were inadequate because the effect of Stokes competition was great and not easily measurable. Thus, they did grant the injunction. — Ermessens-; messbar

II. Injunction

1. General

An injunction directs a party to refrain from doing a particular act. It is especially common in cases where the defendant is sued by his former employer and charged with breaching an employment contract by working for a competitor. — einstweilige Verfügung – anweisen – unterlassen; Arbeitgeber; Wettbewerb

2. Specific Situation: Personal Services Contracts

Courts almost never order specific performance of a contract for personal services. This is true on both sides: the court will not order the employer to resume the employment, nor will it order the employee to perform the services. — Dienstleistung; wiederaufnehmen

But where the employee under an employment contract breaches, the court may be willing to grant an injunction — erlassen preventing him from working for a competitor. The employer must show that the employee's services are unique or extraordinary and that the likely result will not be to leave the employee without other reasonable means of making a living.

hindern

Lumley v. Wagner, 42 Eng. Rep. 687 (1852)

Lumley hired Johanna Wagner, an Opera singer, to sing for a specified time at his opera hall. In the written contract, there was a provision that the singer not perform at any other opera hall. Wagner did not sing for Lumley however, but instead decided to sing for another party. Lumley sued for an injunction to prevent her from singing elsewhere.

einstweilige Verfügung – abhalten

Issue

May a court use an injunction to prevent someone from taking a job from a competitor in order to encourage them to fulfill their obligation to another?

ermutigen

Holding and Reasoning

Yes. As a matter of morals, contractors for personal services should be bound to a true and literal performance of their contract, and not be permitted to breach at their leisure, leaving the other party to the mere chance of damages that a jury may award.

Vergnügen

The court reasoned that since Wagner voluntarily breached, that she should be morally obligated to perform. Although they could not compel the portion of the contract that required her to sing, they could compel the portion that required her not to sing for a competitor.

freiwillig

zwingen

Notes

The opposite point of view is held by Holmes, who believed that a promise to perform was really two alternative promises: one to perform, and one to pay damages in case of breach. Thus, a person

Oliver W. Holmes (1841–1932)
Ass. Justice: 1902-1932
Appointed by: T. Roosevelt

could not truly be morally blameworthy for the failure to perform, they were simply choosing the alternative of paying damages.

III. Limitations on Equitable Remedies

There are three important **limits** on the willingness of the court **to issue either a decree of specific performance or an injunction**.

Grenzen

1. Laches

The equitable defense of laches arises when a party **delays** in bringing an equitable action and the delay prejudices the defendant. Mere delay itself is not a ground for this defense.

billigkeitsrechtlich – Verwirkung – Verspätung

2. Unclean Hands

The unclean hands defense arises when the party seeking specific performance is **guilty of some wrongdoing** in the transaction being sued upon (e.g. the defendant entered into the contract because the plaintiff's lies).
The wrongdoing must be related to the transaction being sued upon: it is not sufficient that the plaintiff has defrauded other persons in similar transactions.

schuldig – Fehlverhalten

Lüge

betrügen

3. Sale to a Bona Fide Purchaser

If the subject matter of a goods or land contract has already been sold to another who **purchased for value and in good faith**, the right to specific performance is cut off.

Diagram 24

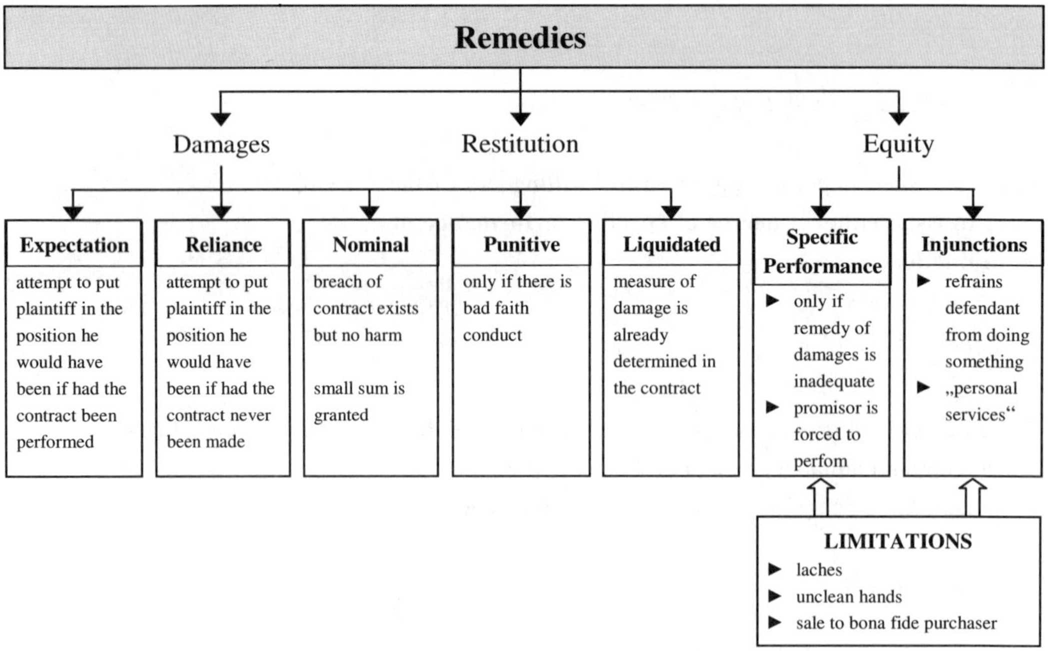

<u>D. Remedies in Quasi Contract</u>

<u>I. Situations</u>

There are a number of situations where **recovery** "on the contract" is **not possible or allowed**:

- situations where there was no <u>attempt</u> even to form a contract, but the **plaintiff <u>deserves</u> some measure of recovery** anyway; — Versuch, Plan; verdienen
- cases where there was an attempt to form a contract, but the **contract is <u>unenforceable</u>** because of statute of frauds, impossibility, illegality, etc.; — nicht durchsetzbar
- cases where there is an enforceable contract, but the plaintiff has materially breached, and therefore may not recover on the contract; and

- cases where the defendant has breached but the plaintiff is not entitled to damages on the contract. — berechtigt

In all of these situations, the plaintiff will often be allowed to recover in **"quasi-contract."**

Cotnam v. Wisdom – Sup. Court of Arkansas, 104 S.W. 164 (1907)

Co-plaintiffs are physicians who performed an emergency surgery in an attempt to save the life of a accident victim who had fallen from a street car. The victim never regained consciousness and later died. The defendant is the administrator of the victim's estate. The plaintiffs are suing for the cost of performing the surgery, which they allege to be customarily dependent on the victim's ability to pay. The defendant claims that since the victim never gained consciousness, there could have been no contract, and further say that the ability of the victim's estate to pay should have no bearing on the value of the services provided.

Arzt – Notoperation
Bewusstsein
Nachlass
behaupten – Opfer
Fähigkeit
keinen Einfluss haben auf

Issue

1. Was there a contract between the unconscious victim and the physicians?, and
2. If so, what was the value of the services they provided?

Holding and Reasoning

1. Yes. A person who receives medical care while in an injured and helpless position is liable for payment by way of implied contract when such medical care is provided in good faith.

Although there was no negotiation, no agreement or "meeting of the minds", these are NOT requirements for the creation of a contract. The physicians provided competent medical care in good faith. The victim received a benefit which requires equitable compensation.

2. The value of medical services rendered to a victim who cannot negotiate is reasonable compensation for the

erhalten – medizinische Versorgung
stillschweigend vereinbarter Vertrag
fähig
angemessener Ersatz

services rendered. The victim could not have contemplated the charges since he was unconscious, and so this is an implied contract without a negotiated price where the only equitable determination of price would be the fair value of the service provided.

Billigkeitsentscheidung – gerechter Wert

II. Unenforceable Contracts

The parties may attempt to form a binding contract which turns out to be unenforceable or avoidable. This may happen because of the Statute of Frauds, mistake, illegality, impossibility, or frustration of purpose. In any of these cases, the court will usually let the plaintiff sue in quasi-contract, and **recover either the value of the services performed (restitution) or plaintiff's reasonable expenditures (reliance)**. Courts almost never award expectation damages in quasi-contract suits.

Schriftformerfordernis

Diagram 25

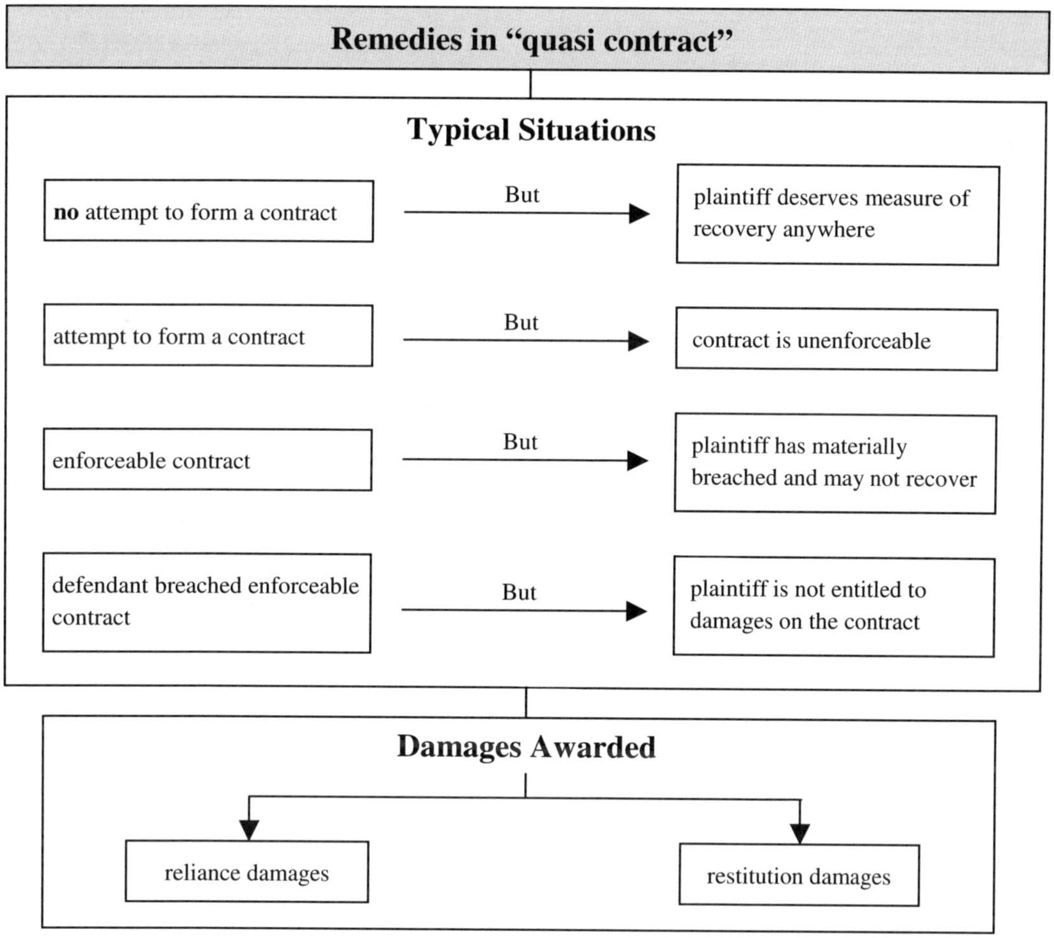
Remedies in "quasi contract"
Typical Situations
no attempt to form a contract
But
plaintiff deserves measure of recovery anywhere
attempt to form a contract
But
contract is unenforceable
enforceable contract
But
plaintiff has materially breached and may not recover
defendant breached enforceable contract
But
plaintiff is not entitled to damages on the contract
Damages Awarded
reliance damages
restitution damages

Vocabulary

– A –

abolish	abschaffen
abortion	Abtreibung
access	Zugriff, Zugang; aufrufen
according	gemäß
account	Konto, Abrechnung
accounting	Buchführung, -haltung
acknowledge	anerkennen, eingestehen
acquittal	Freispruch
act	Gesetz, Erlass
action	Handlung, Prozess
actionable	einklagbar
adjudicate	entscheiden
admit	zugeben, zulassen
admission	Eintritt, Zugeständnis
advice	Rat, Empfehlung
affidavit	schriftliche, unter Eid abgegebene Erklärung
affirm	bestätigen
agency	Stellvertretung
agent	Stellvertreter
agreement	Übereinkunft, Vereinbarung
allegation	Vorbringen, Behauptung
ambassador	Botschafter
amendment	Zusatz, Änderung
annual	jährlich
anti-trust	Antitrust
appeal	Berufung, Revision; Berufung/Revision einlegen
appellate	Berufungs-, Revisions-
apply	beantragen, zeichnen
application	Antrag, Bewerbung
apoint	ernennen
arbitration	Schlichtung
argument	Streit, Beweisführung
arraignment	Aufruf zum Zwecke der Antwort auf die Anklage
articles of incorporation	Gesellschaftsvertrag, Gründungsdokumente

assault	gewaltsame Drohung
assent	Zustimmung
asset	Aktiva, Vermögenswerte
assignment	Abtretung, Übereignung
association	Gesellschaft, Verband, Bund
attorney	Anwalt
authority	Befugnis, Vollmacht

– B –

bail	Kaution, Bürgschaft
ballot	Wahl
bancrupt	bankrott, insolvent
bancruptcy	Bankrott, Konkurs
bar	Anwaltschaft
bargain	Handel, Geschäft
battery	Körperverletzung
bench trial	Gerichtsverfahren ohne Jury
benefit	Nutzen, Vorteil
BFP = Bona Fide Purchaser	gutgläubiger Erwerber
bill	Gesetzesvorlage
board of directors	Vorstand einer AG
board meeting	Vorstandssitzung
bounty	Subvention, Belohnung
breach of contract	Vertragsverletzung
branch	Filiale
brief	Schriftsatz
burden of proof	Beweislast
business	Unternehmen
bylaw	Satzung

– C –

cancel	absagen
candidate	Kandidat
canvass	werben, bearbeiten
capable	fähig, tauglich
capacity	(Rechts-, Geschäfts-) Fähigkeit,
capital	Kapital, Vermögen
case	Fall

cause	Ursache
certificate	Schein, Bescheinigung
certify	bescheinigen, bestätigen, beglaubigen
certiorari denied	Revisionsantrag abgelehnt
chairman	Vorsitzender
charitable corporation	gemeinnützige Körperschaft
civil	bürgerlich, zivilrechtlich
Chief Justice	Vorsitzender des U.S. Supreme Court
claim	Anspruch, Forderung
classify	einteilen, einordnen
client	Mandant
closed corporation	Kapitalgesellschaft mit wenigen Gesellschaftern (ähnlich wie GmbH)
codify	kodifizieren
collateral	nebensächlich
collective	gemeinsam, gemeinschaftlich
collusion	geheimes Einverständnis, Kollusion
commerce	Handel
commercial	Handel-
commission	Kommission, Provision
common law	nicht-kodifiziertes Recht
company	Gesellschaft, Unternehmen
compensation	Entschädigung
compensatory damages	kompensatorischer Schadensersatz
complaint	Beschwerdeschrift, Klageerhebung
compulsory	zwingend
conduct	Verhalten
confirm	bestätigen
conflict of laws	Internationales Privatrecht
Congress	Kongress
consent	Zustimmung, zustimmen
consideration	Gegenleistung, Entgelt
constitution	Verfassung
construe	auslegen
contract	Vertrag
contributory negligence	mitwirkendes Verschulden
co-ownership	Miteigentum
corporate	Gesellschafts-, Unternehmens-
corporation	Kapitalgesellschaft

counterclaim	Gegenanspruch
covenant	Vertragsabrede
creditor	Gläubiger
culpable	strafbar, schuldhaft

– D –

damage	Schaden
deceptive	täuschend, irreführend
defamation	Ehrverletzung, Beleidigung
defect	Fehler
defendant	Beklagter, Angeklagter
defense	Verteidigung
demurrer	Rechtseinwand
denial	Bestreiten, Leugnen
deposition	außergerichtliche schriftliche, eidliche Aussage
detriment	Schaden, Nachteil
director	Direktor, leitender Angestellter
disclaimer	Ablehnung, Verweigerung, Verzicht
discovery	Entdeckung, Offenlegung
discretion	Ermessen
dismiss	abweisen, zurückweisen
donation	Schenkung
draft	Entwurf
due	schuldig, fällig, zahlbar
duress	Zwang, Nötigung
duty	Pflicht

– E –

easement	Grunddienstbarkeit
effective date	Tag des Inkrafttretens
election	Wahl, Abstimmung
employ	anstellen, beschäftigen
employee	Angestellter, Arbeitnehmer
employer	Arbeitgeber
enact	gesetzlich verordnen
encumbrance	Schuldenlast, Belastung
enforcement	Durchsetzung, Erzwingung
equity	Billigkeit, equity-Recht

establish	gründen, errichten, einrichten
estate	Vermögen, Nachlass, Erbmasse
estoppel	Hinderungsgrund, rechtshemmender Einwand
evidence	Beweis
excess	Überschuss, Mehr-
executive	vollziehende Gewalt
exemplary damages	verschärfter Schadensersatz
expiration	Ablauf, Erlöschen, Verfall
extrinsic evidence	Beweis, der nicht aus der Urkunde selbst hervorgeht

– F –

fact	Tatsache
fact-finding	Tatsachenfeststellung
false	falsch, unrichtig, unwahr
fault	Schuld
federal	Bundes-, den Bund betreffend
federation	Föderation
fee	Gebühr
felony	Verbrechen
fiction of law	Rechtsfiktion
fiduciary	Treuhänder
file	Ordner, Sammelmappe; einreichen
filing	Einreichung, Einordnung
fine	Strafe
firm	Firma, Betrieb, Unternehmen
first instance (court of first instance)	erste Instanz
fixture	Einbauten
force	Kraft
foreclose	zwangsvollstrecken lassen
foreclosure	Zwangsvollstreckung
foreseeability	Voraussehbarkeit
forfeit	Verfall, Verwirkung
forum	Gerichtsstand
fraud	Betrug
fraudulent	betrügerisch
fundamental	grundlegend, wesentlich
fund	Fonds, zweckgebundenes Vermögen

– G –

gift	Schenkung, Geschenk
going concern	dynamisches, rentables Unternehmen
good faith	guter Glaube
goods	Waren, Güter
goodwill	Firmenansehen
govern	regieren, bestimmen
government	Regierung
grand jury	Anklagejury
grant	urkundliche Übertragung
gross	brutto
gross negligence	grobe Fahrlässigkeit
guarantee	Garantie, Bürgschaft
guarantor	Bürge
guidelines	Richtlinien
guilt	Schuld

– H –

habitual	gewohnheitsmäßig
hand over	übergeben, überreichen
headquarters	Hauptsitz, Zentrale
hearing	Gerichtsverhandlung
hearsay evidence	Beweis vom Hörensagen
holder	Besitzer
hot pursuit	Nacheile, Verfolgungsrecht

– I –

identify	identifizieren
identity	Identität
i.e.	d.h.
illegal	illegal
illegitimate	unzulässig, unrechtmäßig
illicit	verboten
immovable	unbeweglich
immovables	Immobilie, unbewegliches Vermögen
impeach	unter Amtsanklage stellen
impeachment	Anklage gegen den Präsidenten wegen eines Amtsvergehens

implied	stillschweigend angenommen
import	Einfuhr
impose	verhängen, auferlegen
impossibility of performance	Unmöglichkeit der Leistung
income	Einkommen
incompetent	(geschäfts-) unfähig
incorporate	eine Kapitalgesellschaft gründen
incorporation	Gesellschaftsgründung
increase	Erhöhung, Zunahme
indebted	verschuldet
indefeasible right	unverletzliches Recht
indict	anklagen
indictment	formelle Anklageschrift
indorse	indossieren
inevitable	unvermeidbar
infringement	Verletzung, Übertretung
inherit	erben
injunction	einstweilige Verfügung
injure	verletzen
injustice	Ungerechtigkeit, Unrecht
innocent	unschuldig
insane	geisteskrank
insolvency	Zahlungsunfähigkeit
inspection	Kontrolle, Untersuchung
instance	Instanz
instrument	Urkunde
insult	beleidigen
insurance	Versicherung
intent	Vorsatz
interest	Zinsen
Internal Revenue Service (IRS)	US-Finanzbehörde
intimidate	einschüchtern
intrinsic evidence	aus einer Urkunde abgeleiteter Beweis
invasion of privacy	Verletzung der Privatsphäre
invoice	Rechnung
issue	zu entscheidende Rechtsfrage
item	Artikel, Gegenstand

– J –

joinder	Klagehäufung
joint	Gemeinschaft-, gemeinschaftlich
joint and several	gesamtschuldnerisch
joint tenancy	Gesamthandeigentum
judge	Richter
judgement	Gerichtsurteil
judicature	Gerichtswesen
judicial	richterlich, Gerichts-
judiciary	Judikative
jurisdiction	Jurisdiktion
juror	Schöffe
jury	Geschworene
justice	Gerechtigkeit
justify	rechtfertigen

– K –

know-how	Fachkenntnisse
knowingly	wissentlich, absichtlich
knowledge	Kenntnis, Wissen

– L –

labor	Arbeit
laches	zum Rechtsverlust führendes Versäumnis gesetzlicher Ausschluss- und Versäumnisfristen
lack	Mangel
land	Land
landlord	Vermieter
landowner	Grundbesitzer
lapse of time	Zeitspanne
late	verspätet
law	Gesetz, Recht
lawful	rechtmäßig
law-making	Gesetzgebung
lawsuit	Klage
lawyer	Rechtsanwalt

layman	Laie
lease	Mietvertrag
leasing	Leasing
legal	rechtmäßig
legislate	Gesetze erlassen
legislation	Gesetzgebung
legislature	Legislative
lender	Gläubiger
lessee	Mieter, Pächter
lessor	Vermieter, Verpächter
levy	Steuer, Abgabe
liability	Haftung
liable	haften, haftbar sein
libel	Ehrverletzung
liberty	Freiheit
licence	Konzession, Genehmigung
likelihood	Wahrscheinlichkeit
limit	Grenze
limited liability	beschränkte Haftung
limited liability company	GmbH
limited partnership	Kommanditgesellschaft
litigate	prozessieren
litigation	Prozess, Rechtsstreit
loan	Kredit, Darlehen
lose	verlieren
loss	Verlust

– M –

machinery	Maschinen
mail	Post
maintenance	Erhaltung
majority	Mehrheit, Majorität
malice	Vorsatz
malicious	böswillig
malpractice	ärztlicher Kunstfehler
mandate	Vollmacht
mandatory	obligatorisch
mark	Zeichen, Markierung

matter	Problem, Angelegenheit
measure	Mass
mediate	vermitteln
membership	Mitgliedschaft
mental(ly)	geistig
mercantile law	Handelsrecht
merchantable quality	handelsübliche Qualität
merge	fusionieren
merits of the case	Klagegrund
Michaelmas	29. September, Herbstsitzungsperiode
minor	Minderjähriger
minority	Minderheit
micarriage of justice	Justizirrtum
misconduct	Fehlverhalten, Amtspflichtverletzung
misdemeanour	Vergehen
misuse	Missbrauch
mititagtion	Milderung
mortgage	Hypothek
motion	Antrag
motion to dismiss	Antrag auf Klageabweisung
move	beantragen
movables	Mobilien
municipal	städtisch, kommunal
municipality	Stadtverwaltung
mutual	gemeinsam

– N –

name	Name
naturalization	Einbürgerung
necessaries	Notwendiges
necessity	das Notwendigste (zum Leben)
neglegt	Versäumnis, Unterlassung
negligence	Fahrlässigkeit
negligent	fahrlässig
negotiate	verhandeln
negotiation	Verhandlung
net	netto
nominal	unbedeutend, nominell

nominal damages	geringer Schadensersatz
nomiate	nominieren, aufstellen
nominee	Kandidat
non-profit corporation	gemeinnütziges Unternehmen
notary public	Person, die zur Beurkundung befugt ist (nicht Notar!)
note	Mitteilung, Bescheid
nuissance	Ärgernis
null and void	nichtig, ungültig

– O –

oath	Eid
obey	gehorchen
obedience	Gehorsam
obiter dicta	nicht tragende Entscheidungsgründe
object	Ziel, Zweck
obligate	verpflichtet sein
obligation	Verpflichtung
obsolete	überholt, veraltet
obtain	erhalten, bekommen
occupier	Bewohner
offer	(Vertrags-) Angebot
offeree	Angebotsempfänger
offeror	Anbietender
office	Büro
official	dienstlich, amtlich
omit	auslassen, unterlassen
omission	Unterlassung, Versäumnis
operating	Betrieb
operating budget	Betriebswirtschaftsplan
operation	Geschäft, Tätigkeit
opinion	Meinung, Stellungnahme (eines Gutachters)
opponent	Gegner
oppose	ablehnen, sich widersetzen
option	Option
oral	mündlich
order	Ordnung
ordinance	(städtische) Verordnung
origin	Herkunft

originate	entstehen
outcome	Ergebnis
outline	Überblick, Entwurf
out of court	außergerichtlich
overrule	außer Kraft setzen, aufheben
own	besitzen
owner	Eigentümer
ownership	Eigentum

– P –

panel	
papers	Unterlagen, Dokumente
paragraph	Abschnitt, Absatz
paralegal	Anwaltsassistent
parliament	Parlament
parol	mündlich
parol evidence	mündlicher Beweis
partial	teilweise, Teil-
partner	Gesellschafter, Teilhaber
partnership	Personengesellschaft, offene Handelsgesellschaft
patent	Patent
patented	patentiert
patentee	Patentinhaber
pawn	Verpfändung
pawnbroker	Pfandleiher
pay	bezahlen
payable	zahlbar, fällig
paycheck	Gehaltsscheck
payee	Zahlungsempfänger
payer	Zahler
payment	Zahlung, Begleichung
peace	öffentliche Sicherheit und Ordnung
pecuniary	finanziell
penalty	(Geld-)Strafe
pending	schwebend
pending action	anhängiger Rechtsstreit
pension	Rente, Ruhegehalt
perform	erfüllen, leisten

performance	Ausführung, Erfüllung, Leistung
peril	Gefahr, Risiko
period	Zeitspanne
perjury	Meineid
permission	Erlaubnis, Genehmigung
(in) perpetuity	für immer
personal	persönlich
personal assets	bewegliches Privatvermögen
persanl income	Privateinkommen
personal injury	Körperverletzung
personal service	persönliche Zustellung
petition	Antrag, Klage
petitioner	Antragsteller
plaint	Klage
plaintiff	Kläger
plant	(Maschinen-)Anlage
plead	verteidigen, vorbringen
pleadings	Plädoyers
pledge	Verpfändung, Pfandsache
pledgee	Pfandnehmer
pledger	Verpfänder
policy	Kurs, Linie, Politik, Taktik
politicics	Politik
poll	Wahl, Abstimmung
popular	beliebt
possess	besitzen
possession	Eigentum, Besitz
possessory	besitzrechtlich
postpone	verlagern, verschieben
power	Macht, Kompetenz, Befugnis
preamble	Präamble
precedent	Präzedenzfall
preclude	ausschließen
predecessor	Vorgänger
preferred stock	Vorzugsaktien
pregnancy	Schwangerschaft
preliminary	vorbereitend, vorausgehend
premises	bebautes Grundstück
presidency	Präsidentschaft

presume	annehmen, vermuten
presumption	Vermutung
prima facie	beim ersten Anschein
privacy	Privat-, Intimsphäre
privilege	Sonderrecht, Privileg
privileged documents	der Rechtsverfolgung entzogene Unterlagen
probative	beweiserheblich, beweiskräftig
procedure	Vorgehen, Verfahren
(legal) proceedings	Gerichtsverfahren, Prozess
proceeds	Verkaufserlös
profession	Beruf
profit	Erlös, Gewinn
progress	Fortschritt
prohibit	verbieten, untersagen
prohibition	Verbot
promise	Versprechen
promisee	Versprechensempfänger
promisor	Versprechensgeber
promissory estoppel	Rechtscheinsbindung aufgrund eines Versprechens
promote	(Gesetzesvorlage) einbringen
proof	Beweismittel
poperty	Eigentum
proposal	Vorschlag, Antrag
proprietor	Eigentümer
prosecution	Strafverfolgung, Anklage
protection	Schutz
prove	beweisen
provision	Vorschrift
proxy vote	durch Stellvertreter abgegebene Stimmen
public	öffentlich
public policy	öffentliches Interesse
punish	bestrafen
punitive damages	Strafschadensersatz
purchase	Kauf, Erwerb
purchaser	Käufer
pursuant to	gemäß, laut
pursuit	Verfolgung

– Q –

qualify	berechtigt sein
quarterly	quartalsweise
questioning	Befragung, Verhör
quit	kündigen

– R –

race	Rasse
rate	Satz, Gebühr
real property	Grundbesitz, Grundstück
realty	Grundbesitz, Grundstück
reasoning	Argumentation
receive	erhalten, bekommen
receivables	Forderungen
reciprocal	gegenseitig
reciprocity	Gegenseitigkeit
recognize	erkennen, wiedererkennen
recommendation	Empfehlung
redeem	abzahlen, tilgen
referee	Sachverständiger, Schiedsrichter
register	Verzeichnis, Liste
register of companies	Handelsregister
register of shareholders	Aktienbuch
relief	Klagebegehren
remedy	Abhilfe, Rechtsmittel
rent	Pacht, Miete
reserve	Rücklage
residence	Wohnort
resident	wohnhaft
resign	kündigen
respondeat superior	Deliktshaftung des Auftraggebers für den Beauftragten
restrain order	einstweilige Verfügung
review	Überprüfung
revoke	aufheben, annullieren
revocation	Widerruf, Annullierung
right	Recht, Berechtigung, Anrecht, Anspruch
rule	Regel, Richtlinie; gerichtliche Entscheidung
rule of law	Rechtsstaatsprinzip

– S –

sack	entlassen
safety	Sicherheit
sale	Verkauf
sample	Muster, Probe
schedule	Terminplan
scope	Geltungsbereich
seal	Siegel
search	Suche, Durchsuchung
search warrant	Durchsuchungsbefehl
secret	geheim
Secretary of State	US Außenminister
Secretary of the Interior	US Innenminister
Secretary of the Treasury	US Finanzminister
securities	Wertpapiere
segregation	Rassentrennung
self-defence	Notwehr
seller	Verkäufer
senate	Senat
sentence	Strafe
separation of powers	Gewaltenteilung
service	Zustellung
servient tenement	dienendes Grundstück
severance	Auflösung des Mitbesitzes
share	Aktie
shareholder	Aktionär
shipment	Versand, Verladung
shipping	Versand
signatory	Unterzeichner
sitting	Gerichtssitzung
slander	Verleumdung
sole proprietor	Alleineigentümer
solvent	zahlungsfähig
sovereignty	Souveränität
specimen	Muster, Probe
spouse	Ehegatte
stare decisis	Grundsatz der bindenden Kraft der Präjudizien
State Department	Außenministerium

statute	Gesetz
statute-barred	verjährt
statute of limitations	prozessuales Verjährungsgesetz
stock	Vorrat
Stock Exchange	Wertpapierbörse
subpoena	erzwingen
subsidiary company	Tochtergesellschaft
subsidy	Subvention
substantial	erheblich, beträchtlich
sue	klagen, verklagen
sufferance	Duldung
suit	Zivilprozess, Klage
summary judgment	Urteil im beschleunigten Verfahren

– T –

tangibles	Sachvermögen
tariff	Zolltarife
tax	Steuer
tax-exempt	steuerfrei
tenancy	Miet- oder Pachtverhältnis
tenant	Mieter, Pächter
term	Dauer, Zeitraum
termnate	beenden, auflösen
testify	aussage, bezeugen
total	gesamt
trade	Handel, Gewerbe
trademark	Warenzeichen
trader	Kaufmann
trade union	Gewerkschaft
transcript	Abschrift
treaty	Vertrag, Abkommen
tespass	unbefugtes Betreten
trespass to chattels	Eigentumsstörung
trespasser	jemand, der unbefugt fremdes Land betritt
trial	Gerichtsverhandlung, Prozess
trust	Treuhandschaft
trustee	Vermögensverwalter

– U –

ultra vires	über die Befugnisse hinausgehend
unanimous	einstimmig
unavoidable	zwangsläufig
unconstitutional	verfassungswidrig
unilateral	einseitig
unincoporated association	nicht eingetragener Verein
union	Staatenbund, Zusammenschluss
unjust	unrechtmäßig
unjust enrichment	ungerechtfertigte Bereicherung
unlimited	unbegrenzt
unliquidated damages	nicht festgesetzter Schadensersatzanspruch
unpaid	unbezahlt
unreasonable	unvernünftig, unangemessen
unsecured creditor	Gläubiger ohne Sicherheiten
usage	Sitte, Brauch
use	nutzen, benutzen
usual	normal, gewöhnlich
usurp	sich bemächtigen

– V –

vacant	frei, unbesetzt
valid	begründet, gültig, rechtswirksam
validat	gültig erklären, bestätigen
validity	Gültigkeit
valuable	kostbar, wertvoll
valuables	Wertsachen
value	Wert
value added tax (VAT)	Mehrwertsteuer
vendee	Käufer
vendor	Verkäufer
venue	zuständiger Gerichtsort, Gerichtsstand
verbal	mündlich
verdict	Spruch der Geschworenen
verify	überprüfen
versus (v.)	gegen (in Fallnamen)
vest	Besitz übertragen, ein Recht verleihen
vested interest	sicher begründetes Recht (auf zukünftigen Besitz)

vested remainer	unentziehbares Anwartschaftsrecht
veto	Einspruchsrecht
vicarious	indirekt, stellvertretend
vice	Vize-
violate	verletzen
voidk	ungültig
voidable	aufhebbar
voluntary	freiwillig
vote	Abstimmung
voter	Wähler
vouch for	bürgen für
voucher	Gutschein

– W –

waive	verzichten
waiver	Verzicht, Verzichtserklärung
warranty	Garantie
welfare	Fürsorge
whereas	in Anbetracht der Tatsache, dass
wholesale	Großhandel
willful	mutwillig, vorsätzlich
wind up	beschließen
wind up a company	ein Unternehmen liquidieren
withdraw	abheben, widerrufen
withhold	zurückhalten
witness	Zeuge
writ	gerichtliches Dokument
writ of certiorari	Verfügung, mit der die Revision zugelassen wird
wrongful	unrechtmäßig

Index
